# ANGELS
*Their Mission and Message*

# Angels

## THEIR MISSION AND MESSAGE

CHARLES R. JAEKLE

MOREHOUSE PUBLISHING

Copyright © 1995 Charles R. Jaekle

MOREHOUSE PUBLISHING

EDITORIAL OFFICE:
871 Ethan Allen Highway
Ridgefield, CT 06877

CORPORATE OFFICE:
P.O. Box 1321
Harrisburg, PA 17105

Library of Congress
Cataloging-in-Publication data:

Jaekle, Charles R.
        Angels: their mission, and message / Charles R. Jaekle.
        p.    cm.
        Includes bibliographical references (p.  ).
        ISBN 0-8192-1635-6 (alk. paper)
        1. Angels. 2. Angels — History of doctrines. I. Title
BT966.2.J34  1995
2 3 5'. 3— dc20

                                                          95-22769
                                                          CIP

Printed in the United States of America

FOR MY GRANDCHILDREN:

Alex, Allison, Ashley, Ben,
Casey and Eric

# Table of Contents

# Acknowledgments

Many people helped me in the writing of this book, but I want to give special thanks to those who read and commented on portions of the draft manuscript. The Rev. Karen Stroup and the Rev. Prof. William Stafford helped with various drafts and gave detailed feedback when it was most needed. Other clergypersons also gave valuable assistance: Susan Gresinger, Jacques Hadler, Jim Hall, Edward Morgan, Dale Ostrander, Jim Petty, Benjamin Pratt and Robert Whitten. Abby Donovan, Adele and Richard Pogue, with Betty and Hugh Charlton, along with my son Stephen Jaekle, my brother Richard Jaekle, and my niece Nancy Jaekle, helped me clarify my thoughts and my writing. Anne Burke provided unfailing secretarial assistance. My editor, Deborah Grahame-Smith, strongly supported the entire project, turning her keen eye on each page. Ann, my wife, gave me important help in every phase of this book's development while giving me a loving home to share.

Springfield, Virginia                              Charles Jaekle
April 19, 1995

# Angels Underground

A recent edition of the Phil Donahue talk show featured a small panel of men and women who reported on their extraordinary and vivid encounters with angels. There was a breathlessness about it all. As each telling followed the preceding one, its narrator seemed to be saying, "Wow, listen to this one!" Granted that an angel did enter the lives of these people, each angel experience was related in such a way as to be isolated and encapsulated. God was mentioned only in passing, their church not at all, and the transforming power of the encounter was marked only insofar as it reminded us that the universe might include more than what science can describe. Much popular angelology is, indeed, an angelology of exclamation—and, with nowhere else to go and nothing else to say, dead-ended.

An astonishingly large number of men and women today do have a religious conviction that includes a belief in angels. The 1993 Christmas edition of *Time* magazine displayed a beautiful young female angel on its front cover, announcing its feature article: "The New Age of Angels: 69% of Americans believe they exist. What in heaven is going on?" The article tells us that Hillary Clinton, who has an angel pin she wears on days she needs help, said that angels would be the theme of the White House Christmas tree in 1993. There was a rising fascination with angels, the article declared. Angels had a vast constituency and were riding an astonishing crest of interest everywhere in the United States. The phenomenon, its writer said, was "a grass roots revolution of the

1

spirit in which all sorts of people are finding all sorts of reasons to seek answers about angels for the first time in their lives."

The article agreed, however, with the observation that the fascination was more popular than theological. Sophy Burnham, author and lecturer on angels and very much in demand to speak on that subject, told the *Wall Street Journal* in an earlier edition that ordinary people were starving for information about angels but they were not getting it from traditional sources, including their own churches and synagogues.

Ms. Burnham is certainly accurate in that appraisal. Angels are, indeed, amazingly popular, but I, for one, cannot recall one sermon on that subject I ever preached, or ever heard anyone else preach, in all my years within the Christian church. Nor do I remember a lecture, or even an informal discussion, within the walls of any church where I have assisted or belonged that included a serious interest in angels or the church's position on that subject. Further, I cannot recall, even once, in my entire theological education in preparation for the ordained ministry or in any postgraduate study, any discussion having to do with angels or the church's historic angelologies. Reflection on a lifetime of church membership leads to one conclusion: a massive bias that angels and their encounters with human beings are unworthy of serious religious study or investigation.

My own interest in angels unfolded slowly over several months. It began when the large counseling agency where I have labored, The Pastoral Counseling and Consultation Centers of Greater Washington, advertised a short lecture series titled "Wrestling with Angels." The series was wildly popular, and the classes quickly filled with agency clients and others in the metropolitan Washington community. The enthusiasm with which the subject of angels was greeted provoked my attention. How, of all things, was it possible for angels to generate the interest they assuredly did?

I recalled that I have had clients who spoke to me of their belief in angels and who told me about experiences with them. One client, an older woman, told me of a time when she was driving home from work in heavy traffic during a snowstorm. Her car hit a patch of ice and went into a spin. She braced herself for a collision, but miraculously her car spun to the side of the road away from oncoming traffic. She told me that she was delivered by the hand of God, in the form of an angel who saved her life. A young man told me that he had tested HIV positive. Bewildered and humiliated, he saw his life in ruins. One week later he was informed that his test results were questionable and he must be retested. He subsequently learned that he was not HIV positive at all. He credited this good news to the ministry of his guardian angel.

I have held my congregational membership in St. Mark's Episcopal Church in Washington, D.C., for nineteen years, regularly assist at Holy Communion, and occasionally preach and teach in the adult Sunday school. St. Mark's communicants know me and, I think, like and trust me. When it became known that I was interested in angels, I was introduced to an extraordinary phenomenon, one with which I have since become increasingly familiar. Four members either sent me a note or telephoned to explain that they required my pledge of confidence, because, although they had experienced an encounter with an angel that had changed their lives, they were fearful their experience might "leak out" into the congregation and they would be embarrassed by the disclosure. Two of them expressed the conviction that in the congregational environment of St. Mark's they might be thought to be in need of psychiatric care. Three of the four had read Sophy Burnham's book and were grateful for the support it provided in letting them know that other persons, who were not considered odd or abnormal in any way, had had similar experiences.

These four parishioners—and I will not dare to speculate on how many others—had gone underground with their angels. A colleague, a member of the clergy in a different denomination, reported that she had occasion to teach a Wednesday evening adult discussion group at a small suburban church. The subject of angels was mentioned by a participant. Most class members scoffed. During the next week, quite unexpectedly, five persons from that class called to tell the pastor privately about their experiences with angels. Angels, it seems, do address a sizeable population, but that population is fearful that the encounter may be considered intellectually disreputable by the educated public at large and within their mainline churches.

Although severed from ecclesiastical concern or notice, belief in angels and experiences with them have flourished nonetheless. Angels have never been formally renounced by any church body. Belief or interest in them simply atrophied. Angels became, then, the domain of individual interest—a large spiritual underground, a folk spirituality where angel experiences occur unattended and unaddressed either by theological reflection or a pastoral ministry.

Vitally important questions beg for answers. How did it come about that our churches and seminaries lost interest in angels, and why, despite that loss of ecclesiastical interest, do angels continue their personal popularity? A central focus for this book will be how and why this state of affairs developed, its consequences for individual and corporate spiritual growth, and what might be done to bring angelology into the church's mainstream again. The church, especially in the United States, has allowed deep and powerfully religious experiences, once the realm of its pastoral concern, to fall into a vacuum. The effect of this withdrawal has been the growth of an angelology estranged from a more enlightened and integrated theological perspective and severed from the churc h ' s pastoral care.

Christians, especially those who choose to ignore angels, need to be reminded that their heritage is drenched with references to angels. The Bible, both Old and New Testaments, is saturated with stories about angels. All the biblical authors took angels seriously and expected their readers to do likewise. Some of our most familiar hymns celebrate angels as we join with them in praise and thanksgiving:

> Hark! The herald-angels sing,
> "Glory to the new-born King!
> Peace on earth, and mercy mild,
> God and sinners reconciled."

Joyful all ye nations rise,
Join the triumph of the skies;
With th' angelic host proclaim,
Christ is born in Bethlehem!

The earliest Christian theologians, including St. Augustine, believed in angels and considered them essential actors in God's providential will for humankind and the world. Later, in the thirteenth century, the theologian Thomas Aquinas, whose writings were declared by papal decree to be authoritative for the Catholic faithful, was known as the "Angelic Doctor," not only because of the power and subtlety of his theological thinking, but because a substantial part of the corpus of his writing was given to the subject of angels. Karl Barth, possibly the most important Protestant theologian of the twentieth century, thought it essential to devote two chapters of his prodigious *Church Dogmatics* to angelology—169 closely packed pages of theological discourse, including a detailed historical exposition of angelology in the Western church.

The very large gap between the angelology espoused by the church's most prestigious thinkers and its later ecclesiastical neglect requires a bridge, and this book will attempt to provide one. This gap represents important losses, not only for those who experience an angel visitation but for the church as well.

The men and women I interviewed report that their angel visit touched them at the center of their personhood and was transforming. There was a regeneration of hope, a sense of newness. What had been life threatening or deeply disappointing was, somehow, changed. This spiritual inward transformation, however, was for many of them incomplete. They felt that something further needed to be done—something had to be connected and confirmed. Most were at least modestly faithful church members, but they felt their angel experience cut them off even further from congregational participation. The writer of the Fifty-First Psalm pleads, "Create in me a clean heart, O God, and put a new and right spirit within me." The psalmist expresses the yearnings of countless generations of believers; yet the resources and comforts of the Christian tradition may be lost to those who currently do experience the newness the psalmist longs to know.

In its past the church has been more than hospitable to those men and women whom angels visit, and it has offered much. It developed a pastoral ministry that brought to bear the wisdom of many generations in its care for those whose lives had been touched and transformed. Without that ministry and in the church's current dissociated condition, angel encounters may lose vitality, become inflated or trivialized, in some cases distorted, and in many of their expressions, spiritually attenuated.

Churches and congregations, on the other hand, need a witness of God's presence in the world that reaches into the depth of our human experience. Angels are such a witness. Viewed biblically and through a theological lens, both Catholic and Protestant alike, angels and their encounter with men and women are a testimony to God's creative power in communion with the human beings whom he created and loves. Yet the spiritual energy of that witness, neither claimed nor celebrated, is lost to our churches in their persistent neglect of their own legacy.

In summary, the backbone of this book is the fact that a large number of men and women today report angel visitations and testify to their life-transforming power. At the same time, their experience is often expressed furtively, as if it were odd, "off the wall"; it is shared reluctantly, if at all, within most congregations, and least reluctantly in a nonchurch setting. The church's own angelologies, largely neglected, have fragmented and then migrated to an underground to become a "folk" angelology where it exists in a dissociated condition. Churches, along with their various institutions, find themselves cut off not only from a potent and popular spirituality but from the promise of a powerful witness to God's love and care for all his creation.

Many contemporary studies of religious or spiritual matters written in the United States are exercises in psychology or sociology. I do not intend this inquiry to be a psychological analysis of conversion experiences or any other kind of spiritual experiences. I do not write as a psychologist or sociologist of religion, but as a Christian believer who struggles with his own angelology. Compared with other angel experiences represented here, my own personal experience has been undistinguished—undramatic, less vivid, and more given to an interpretation as an experience other than an angel encounter. As I reflect on the interviews I have had with those who told me of their angel experiences, I have come more and more to appreciate those events coalescing around my father's death as the grace of God, which allowed an angel to speak to me through the voice of my very human psychotherapist.

I quickly came to understand that my interviews with those men and women whom angels visit were stressful for them, as well as for me. My interviewees were attempting to describe an intense personal experience with words and concepts inadequate to the task. There are vocabularies available for the description of inner, psychological changes, and most of those interviewed could easily communicate their psychological experiences. They might say, "The angels made me so happy I cried," or that the encounter was "an inner joy" or "a flood of relief." The stress was aroused in proportion to their attempt to describe the other part of the experience—the angel.

Most of the men and women with whom I worked simply dismissed all the awkwardness they might have felt about who and what an angel is, by refusing to speculate or by a flat-out assertion of the impossibility of the encounter—yet it is a reality nonetheless—and that was that. Some attempted to make an explanation of the angel appearance, and this precipitated a noticeable unease in both speaker and listener: in the speaker because the explanation seemed to put their incredibly valuable angel experience in a markedly poor and fragile container; and in me because I found myself, in some cases, incapable of following their explanation without resisting it, or even fighting with it, when doing so was, under the circumstances, neither decent nor appropriate.

The stress level, however, seemed to rise sharply when we discussed the subject of sharing their angel experiences either with their families or with their church. As an Episcopal priest and a representative of the church, I was approached with some ambivalence, although my readiness to take the experience on its own terms seemed reassuring. Some of the men and women interviewed refused to consider the possibility of making their experience known to their church or, even, to their own pastor. All of them were hesitant, but a majority gave the impression that, given support from a credible source, they might be willing to tell their pastors what it was the angel did for them. Their feelings were somewhat more mixed when it came to their own families, although with some picking and choosing among family members, they could be persuaded to confide their experiences. It is a telling statistic, nonetheless, that very few of them ever ventured to do so.

Two years after it came to be known within my own church and among professional colleagues that I was interested in angels, referrals were made to me from parish clergy by pastoral counselors with a professional practice, and one client was referred by a psychiatrist. In addition, then, to those men and women I interviewed who reported an angel visitation, I had a small group of clients who were in therapy, with me in a setting appropriate for a more in-depth pastoral study of how their angel experiences affected their lives and how a more communal and pastoral ministry might help them.

Those who shared their angel experiences presented me with a remarkable variety of such encounters. Some angels appeared in a vision or a dream. Others were not seen but heard. Four of those interviewed told me of flesh-and-blood human beings who were angels—most of them strangers, although one interviewee knew that person in her day-to-day life. They were perceived as both male and female angels, the majority female. All the angels were imposing, even commanding figures, and with few exceptions, beautiful. Why this is so remains a mystery. The exceptions occurred, as in my own personal experience, when the angel appeared as a human being. In any case, there is an assortment of angels and angel encounters, and when I extend myself to treat them all with appreciation and respect, there is much to learn and much to enjoy.

Much current angelology is exorbitantly individualistic.

There is very little communal participation, even friendship sharing for many who have had an angel experience. Theirs is an individualism moving toward isolation—a condition induced by the detachment of angels and angel encounters from their theological and congregational roots and reinforced by the individualistic bias of American spiritual expression. This particular quality of our contemporary religious life will occupy an important place in my main focus. Harold Bloom sees a common thread through the many forms of American religious life. He believes there is such a thing as American religion and that it has kept the figure of Jesus a very solitary and parochial Jesus.[1] The quintessential hymn that expresses that spirit is "I come to the garden alone," where "he walks with me and he talks with me and he tells me I am his own." Bloom identified much of this spirituality as excessively private and personal, and that judgment is one I share. For many Christians the church is a voluntary association of individuals who convene weekly but who stubbornly exist as individuals responsible to God on their own. This prompts an inquiry into the cultural and philosophical vectors that give rise to this bias and an exploration of the spiritual forms it produces.

Most personal conversions or transformations include movement *into* a communal setting. There the formation of relationships with persons who share similar experiences enhances self-esteem and offers nurture and support and, equally important, provides confirmation and consolidation of the transforming event. The Evangelical faithful celebrated that reality in a well-known hymn written more than two hundred years ago:

> Blest be the tie that binds
> Our hearts in Christian love;
> The fellowship of kindred minds
> Is like to that above.

> We share our mutual woes,
> Our mutual burdens bear;
> And often for each other flows
> The sympathizing tear.

Those who experience angels know that their encounter is often perceived as very strange. They know too that this precious spiritual encounter moves *them* toward isolation. Their struggles are not shared, and there is little fellowship of kindred minds.

The result of this unconnected state for both the church and for those whom angels visit will occupy much discussion in this book. However, one painful aspect of it is certainly the lonely vulnerability to a psychiatric or psychological diagnosis that many feel once their angel encounter is revealed.

Much of the psychological literature that explores intense religious experience is psychoanalytic in nature. It proceeds from the view that the crisis precipitating that experience is derived from a deficiency generated out of fear, loneliness, or desperation of some sort. This produces, then, a mindset and the vocabulary of deficit used by psychotherapists, and perhaps even pastoral counselors. They may see an angel encounter as, primarily, a search for emotional resolution, and those who have such experiences may be diagnosed either as mentally ill or, at least, as emotionally immature.

The mental health of clients and those I interviewed who reported angel encounters seemed remarkably similar to that of others in my practice and to the general population I know. They seemed neither more nor less afflicted with the trials and tribulations of everyday life: their marriages, health problems, career difficulties, and the stresses and tragedies life offers. The most noticeable difference was the carefulness, bordering on secretiveness, with which many of them approached their angel experience. Other clients might be extraordinarily wary about sexual interests or experiences, about their money, or about certain misadventures in their past, but few are as undisclosing about a religious matter. Nonetheless, such caution did not seem to me, on that account, to translate into a more noticeably dysfunctional mental state than for others.

The language of deficit, of diagnosis and illness, is, however, everywhere, both inside and outside our congregations. Psychologist Kenneth Gergen writes:

As psychiatrists and psychologists try to explain undesirable behavior, they generate a technical vocabulary of deficit. This language is slowly disseminated to the public at large, so that they too can become conscious of mental health issues. As people acquire the vocabulary, they also come to see self and others in these terms.... The new vocabulary enters the culture, engendering still further perceptions of illness, and so on, in a continuous spiral of infirmity.[2]

Vocabularies used to describe an angel experience may be vastly different from that used in psychotherapy or counseling. Angel language abounds in dramatic extravagance. It is wildly affirming, the language of personal transformation, of rhapsody, ecstasy. In their isolated condition, those whom angels visit are indeed subject to the suspicion that they are somehow odd and perhaps in need of "treatment."

Nonetheless, certain identifiable characteristics of those whom angels visit are readily apparent. Every person interviewed had some sort of relationship with the Christian church, with its worship, and with its message. Some were nominal church members who circulated along the periphery of congregational life. Others had been members and, for various reasons, left. A few were fervent in their responsibilities as church members.

All of my clients and interviewees were, in some fashion, theists—that is, they said they believed in God or knew that God existed, or said they trusted in God and that they held this conviction before their angel encounter. For some of them, thoughts about God and the Divine had become a vague spirituality with little content and without focus. For others, their theism was either comfortably within the tradition of the Hebrew-Christian faith or approaching it. None of those I interviewed was an outright atheist prior to their angel experience, and every one reported a kind of philosophical readiness for such an experience because, as one interviewee said, "I never doubted we live in a spiritual world for one moment." Others

might agree with John Milton that millions of spiritual creatures walk the earth unseen, both when we are awake and when
we sleep.

All the subjects for this study reported a personal crisis
prior to their angel experience: a fearful medical diagnosis, a
life-threatening accident, a failing marriage, or some other
extraordinary, stressful event or situation. At such times their
usual repertory of coping strategies had failed and they felt
alone, very unsure of themselves, and vulnerable. The crisis
precipitated a disorientation in their lives, and the angel met
them at the boundary of their human capacities. Angels, it
seems, appear to those who need them and who make room to
receive their presence.

It should be acknowledged that encounters with angels
share a common predicament with other expressions of personal faith in our present cultural and intellectual climate. For
centuries our Judeo-Christian culture exhibited thought
forms that interconnected. The seams between the church's
theology and its secular expressions were so tightly interlaced
as to be all but invisible. Not so today. The laces have broken
and the seams are wider and widening. We do not intercon-
nect, as in a party line where all the elements of our society
want to talk and interrupt each other.

Our expressions of personal spiritual life, including our
experiences with angels, may be likened to floating ice fragments on a large lake which scarcely touch. There is a community of religious folk who have such experiences, but their
difficulty is that their vocabulary does not connect with the
vocabulary of those who do not have them.

When the seams open and the fragments move farther
apart, we move into a state of far-reaching ferment.
Everywhere we experience the dilemma of identity and the
shocks of dislocation. But while such fragmenting may have
disoriented us, it has also made space for new ways of thinking and communicating. Most particularly, it may now be possible to lay the foundation for a theological view of angels that
does not depend on either a crass supernaturalism or a sus-
pension of our intellectual facilities, and *Angels: Their
Mission and Message* will reach for such a position. I will not

attempt to philosophize about angels and angel appearances, but I will certainly suggest ways they can be viewed that give credence to their spiritual power and a testimony for God's providential presence in our world.

Finally, I am wistfully aware of the aesthetics of angelology. A historical anthology of paintings or poetry whose subject is angels makes a stunning display. Angels do give themselves handsomely to all the artistic forms, and I will use these from time to time to comment on certain spiritual intentions and meaning. There is a sense of inevitability, a vindication in artistic magnificence, uniquely so, when it includes angels. It is reported that Karl Barth imagined that angels, left to themselves, have the exquisitely good taste to play Mozart and that the Lord enjoys listening to them.

It is my expectation that all those who persevere through the descriptions and discernments of this book will be enriched and their lives enlarged. However, it is not my purpose merely to exclaim over those who wrestle with an angel, but to encourage and enfranchise them. I hope to reconnect their angel encounter with a larger understanding of God's purpose, while I embolden our churches to reclaim their ancient legacy. It is of vital importance that the churches do so, not only for their own theological health, but because the men and women who experience the transforming events this book describes need theological integration, congregational support, and, above all, the church's pastoral care.

*Notes*

1. See Harold Bloom, *The American Religion: The Emergence of the Post-Christian Nation* (New York: Simon and Schuster, 1992).

2. Kenneth R. Gergen, *The Saturated Self: Dilemmas of Identity in Contemporary Life* (New York: Basic Books, 1991), 14-15.

# CHAPTER I

# An Abandoned Legacy

Philip told his story hesitantly, with great intensity of feeling, searching my face for any sign of disparagement or disapproval. He said he was nearing his seventieth birthday and that the event that changed his life forever had happened fifty years before, when he was a newly minted second lieutenant in the United States Air Force. He was preparing himself for combat as a fighter pilot and had just completed his course in aerial acrobatics. He was a self-assured, even cocky young man, he said, and when he set out to fly alone at night to Jacksonville, Florida, 190 miles away, he was sure he had set his altimeter to sound an alarm when his aircraft flew below 3,500 feet; he had, in fact, mistakenly set it at 200 feet.

The flight to Jacksonville was pleasant and uneventful. He was refueled and began his flight for his home field, which he approached at 2:00 A.M. Four miles out, he said, he felt frisky enough to attempt a celebration by doing a figure eight, believing that he was well above 3,500 feet since his alarm had not sounded; when it did sound, he was confident he had sufficient altitude to complete his maneuver and level off. He rolled back his canopy as he leveled out, when he heard a voice telling him to look off his right wing. The voice spoke a second time and immediately afterward again, this time in a commanding, masculine voice. He obeyed the command, looked, and was horrified to see, just three feet beneath him, the furrows of a newly plowed field. Sure he was about to crash into that field, he began to scream. What flashed into his mind in that fraction of a second was the thought that his death would be very quick and his mother needn't worry because it wouldn't hurt. At that instant, he said, a powerful force—as if from outside himself—invaded his body so that he was able to respond with a superhuman effort. He pulled back on his controls and calculated that he had cleared the trees on the edge of the field by no more than six inches. He arrived back on his home field shaken to his core, climbed down from the cockpit, slumped to the ground, and cried.

Philip said he could remember every moment of that experience as if it had happened yesterday. He was a completely different man afterward than he was before, he said, because he had proof that he had been blessed. God had sent an angel, probably his guardian angel, to save his life when he was sure that he was going to die. He said, further, that he has since felt a strong obligation—a commitment to the Lord—because he said, "God looked out for me and there had to be some purpose in it." He has been on the alert, he confided, to see what it is he has been called upon to do; and, looking back over the years, he has refocused his life any number of times in response to what he saw as God's direction for him. As a businessman, the owner of a moderate-sized grocery chain, he has found many opportunities to give back to others some of what God had given him.

There has been no motivation to "witness" to this event. Until now, Philip has told no one except his wife and brother and has felt no call from God "to prove or justify it." He said that it never occurred to him to discuss the episode with his pastor or with any group in his church, because he did not want to become "a salesman for it." The important thing was that the episode had happened as he said. It was a "fact" and "the blessing of grace is its own belief."

Jane told me her story in a long, detailed letter. She explained that she was in her first year as a seminary student when she awoke at 3:30 in the morning to find an angel standing at the foot of her bed. The angel was female, had no wings, was uncommonly tall, and appeared to be half black and half Asian. The most remarkable feature of the angel was her lack of hair; instead, flames that flickered and moved seemed to be coming out of her head.

Jane said she wasn't afraid at all; it was as if a tiny part of her had always known this angel existed and would, one day, visit her. The angel's voice was very loud as she said, "I've come to tell you how much God loves you." Immediately Jane felt "a wave of love," an experience, she said, of being completely, totally, and unconditionally loved. It was a feeling of being aligned with and awakened to the central truth of who God is and "what all this is supposed to be about." The angel spoke, then, a second time, saying, "You know, Jane, you are perfectly free." At that moment, Jane knew she could do whatever she needed to do, which, she said, "would change nothing about the way God regarded me."

At the time the angel spoke to her, Jane was seriously considering becoming a nun, spending a disciplined religious life, safe, she said, physically, emotionally, and in every other way. Jane's experience with her angel realigned her life direction. She decided to risk more—much more. Jane believes that when the angel spoke to her, she seemed to be in some kind of spiritual retreat. The message the angel brought to her moved her, "out here," where it is not safe and where she can fail and be hurt. "I am not as happy as I was before the angel came to visit me, but I've discovered that happiness was a pale sort of thing compared to what's out here."

Jane decided to finish her seminary training and to seek ordination, enter graduate school for a Ph.D., let her hair grow longer, begin dancing again, and open herself to the possibility of a relationship with a man. "I know," she said, "that many people's experience with angels is that the angel brings them to safety; mine was just the opposite. Most of us live in a dangerous world and need to be pulled to safety. I was in safety and pushed into danger. Am I glad? Yes, I have had some failures and I have been hurt, but, yes, I can't say I would have it any other way."

Jane is not defensive about her angel encounter, but she is protective. She has, in confidence, discussed it with a spiritual director, and she has shared the experience with a very few trusted friends. She has not discussed the encounter with rector or pastor of any congregation in which she was a member.

"If I told them an angel had come to me, they might well have thought me crazy and referred me for psychological treatment."

Philip's and Jane's experiences with their angels were intense and life transforming. Both identified themselves as Christian—devout Christians, no less—and both found themselves in an exceedingly exposed and lonely position. Their most powerful spiritual experience did not fit the theological or philosophical assumptions of either their churches or their neighbors. Rather, each encounter would be considered an isolated event, likely to be ignored or reduced to a pathology. Their dilemma is further compounded because the more vivid and dramatic the angel encounter, the more likely the experience would be framed as a personal abnormality. The mainline and liberal Protestant churches to which Philip and Jane belong might then unthinkingly adopt a diagnostic posture, devaluing the substance of the experience while extending a "healing" ministry to a supposedly distraught parishioner. This possibility, and their determination to protect their spiritual experiences from that fate, propelled Philip and Jane into isolation. There they confront the assumptions of a culture that considers their experiences to be either the mistaken notion of a crude supernaturalism or the fanaticism of an overheated religious conviction. Philip and Jane find themselves between an anxious or disinterested church and a skeptical, even hostile culture.

There are numerous and complex reasons for this state of affairs. Some are buried in the fabric of the religious and philosophical traditions that we will examine in other chapters. But there are more immediate reasons. Angels depicted in American popular culture are not intellectually reassuring. Images of angels appear everywhere—on wedding and bereavement cards, calendars, posters, stationery. They appear in movies, usually at Christmastime, and are mentioned in a surprising number of pop tunes. A poster announcing a concert by Nirvana shows a splendidly proportioned and scantily clad female angel with wings. Most angels are shown as female, with white robes that reach to their ankles. Their hair is long and flowing, and their eyes are turned upward, as they peer into another and different world.

Surveys of popular attitudes toward angel encounters, which are to be found both inside and outside the church, reveal four main points of view: the Aesthetic, the Supernatural, the Realistic, and the Psychological. These four perspectives, by and large, encompass the vast majority of how nominal and fervent believers, as well as nonbelievers, might think of angels and angel experiences when they think of them at all.

The **Aesthetic** considers angels to be a culturally artful fantasy, like Santa Claus. They constitute a poetic notion handed down to us as a useful tradition, expressing ideas of generosity and gift giving in the spirit of Christmas. Therefore, a harsh deconstruction of that fantasy would be deplored as Scrooge-like or even ridiculed as a premature rupture of childhood innocence. Just as a fourteenth century picture of an angel adoring a Madonna was a culturally valuable fantasy for its own time, it is aesthetically valuable for ours. Such a picture is tenderly beautiful, deeply moving, and deserves an honored position in our cultural heritage.

The Aesthetic viewpoint also acknowledges that not to believe in anything, to see through everything, might be a peculiarly stupid way to cheat oneself. Notions such as angels should be honored, not because we believe in them, but because we grow tired of the predictabilities of daily life. Angels may contribute to brightening and energizing the drabness of everyday existence.

Philip's and Jane's experiences contribute a vividness, a sense of anticipation, even excitement, to the regularities of life. There is no need to think of angels or angel encounters as "real." They may be viewed as "real" by the subjects who experience them, but intelligent persons need not agree. Intelligent and even mildly religious persons can participate in stories of angel encounters without intellectual compromise by embracing as wholesome the intent of the encounter along with its energizing dynamic.

The **super** part of the **Supernatural** view conforms to the idea that there is a special realm of spiritual existence distinct from the ordinary world. Angels and other spiritual beings belong to this supernatural world and interact from time to time with our thoughts, and appear as well, face-to-face in bodily form.

Adherents of the Supernatural position usually think of angel encounters as they do other psychic phenomena, including telepathy, experiences with ghosts, "near death experiences," and the possibility of communicating with the dead. There is a place above and beyond the day-to-day reality we know, which is accessible in dreams or under special circumstances, especially to children, saints, primitive people, and certain persons who have special spiritual gifts.

Some scientists consider belief in a supernatural world to be the defining characteristic of all religion. Accepting this view of religion as normative, Abraham Maslow, a psychologist and influential commentator on religious subjects, writes:

> There is...a road which all profoundly "seriously ultimately concerned" people of good will can travel together for a very long distance. Only when they come almost to the end does the road fork so that they must part in disagreement...only, it seems, [with] the concept of supernatural beings or of supernatural laws or forces; and I must confess my feeling that by the time this forking of the road has been reached, this difference doesn't seem to be of any great consequence except for the comfort of the individual himself. Even the social act of belonging to a church must be a private act, with no great social or political consequences, once religious pluralism has been accepted.[1]

Maslow here discloses a central difficulty with the Supernatural position. The super in supernaturalism opens itself to being understood as "imaginary" and reduced to a kind of comforting religious hobby, "with no great social or political consequences." The natural, on the other hand, may be viewed as the real world distinct from the religious and imaginary one, but it is a world without transcendent or spiritual meaning, an inanimate collection of resources that we can exploit however we like.

The **Realistic** point of view upends the supernatural position. It draws our attention to the assertion that angels may be beautiful, or useful in that they depict important dimensions of life such as goodness, mercy, compassion, and so on, but holds that they are not "real" and do not exist. A grasshopper *Orthopterous*, suborder, *Saitatoria* is real in a way that an angel is not. The grasshopper can be weighed and measured and its bodily parts described, catalogued, and analyzed. There are scientific rules for the designation of something as " real," and angels do not conform to the requirements of demonstrable fact.

Both the proponents and opponents of the supernatural and realistic views share the common understanding that a somewhat neat separation of religious and scientific, spiritual and secular, spirit and body, subject and object, is normative and unquestioned. I will have more to say about these assumptions in a later chapter, but it is enough to note here that they are increasingly viewed by a new generation of philosophy as intellectually insupportable and functionally disastrous.

The fourth point of view, the **Psychological**, holds that angels—along with other mythical creatures—are projections from our interior psychological landscape. Scrooge, the old reprobate in Dickens's *Christmas Carol*, refused to believe in the Ghost of Marley even though the Ghost appeared before his very eyes. The Ghost asks Scrooge why he doubts his own senses. "Because," says Scrooge, "a little thing affects them. A slight disorder of the stomach makes them cheats. You may be an undigested bit of beef, a blot of mustard, a crumb of cheese, a fragment of an underdone potato. There's more of gravy than of the grave about you, whatever you are ! "[2]

A contemporary and less whimsical expression of the Psychological view is found in the position of the noted Jungian psychoanalyst and theorist Murray Stein. Images and visions come from the unconscious and are projected into historical and natural events, much like projections onto a moving picture screen. Dr. Stein writes:

> We live in a post-mythological age in which "God is dead," as Nietzsche proclaimed at the turn of the last century. The myth of God "out there" in space somewhere, a personified parent figure who cares for us and looks after us as His children and sometimes punishes us for our bad ways, is an image that may give comfort to some but is hard to reconcile with our other cognitive maps. Such images, we know or believe we know, are the by-products of archetypal structures projected into the heavens. We now read these images for their psychological meaning—what do they tell us about the state of the psyche?...Visions no longer give us information about the "beyond" but about the psyche.[3]

These projections have a necessary communication function, as one way our unconscious communicates with other parts of ourselves. Angels are not real in the ordinary sense of that word, say the Jungians, but they may be important, since without their appearance in dreams and visions we would be deprived of corrective and enriching information about our lives, being either out of touch or out of balance.

These four positions—Aesthetic, Supernatural, Realistic, and Psychological—are the popular residue of a long philosophical development in our Western culture. They may lie at oblique angles to each other, but they bear a common characteristic. Each is obsessed, in its own way, with the problem of what is "real" and "not real." The Aesthetic assumes that angels are "not real" but are useful adornments; the Supernatural offers the thought that they are "real," but only in their own and different world; the Realistic, that angels do not really exist; and the Psychological view assumes the "unreality" of angels but declares that to be irrelevant to their therapeutic contributions.

Each of these positions carries unspoken assumptions about the nature of the "self" that encounters the angel. The Supernatural implies a tripartite person composed of a mind, a body, and a soul. The soul is often identified with a "real" self that temporarily occupies the body until death, when it returns to God for a final disposition. The Realistic, along with the canons of science, concludes that selves are detached spectators in a world of objects and events. The Psychological posits a richly endowed self bearing the residue of our long evolutionary past, which then imposes human meanings on an indifferent world. The Aesthetic can view selves from any one or a combination of these positions.

The question of what it is to be a self generates perplexities. We seem to know what a self is until we are asked to explain it. We then find ourselves in the dilemma familiar to Alice when she answers the Caterpillar's question, "Who are you?"

> This was not an encouraging opening for a conversation. Alice replied, rather shyly, "I— I hardly know, Sir, just at present—at least I know *who* I was when I got up this morning, but I think I must have been changed several times since then."
>
> "What do you mean by that?" said the Caterpillar sternly. "Explain yourself!" "I can't explain myself, I'm afraid, Sir," said Alice, "because I'm not myself, you see." "I don't see," said the Caterpillar.
>
> Lewis Carroll, *Alice's Adventures in Wonderland*

Complexities abound. Each of the thought patterns identified with the Aesthetic, Supernatural, Realistic, and Psychological perspectives assumes in its own way a "self" that is separated or detached from its world. We will examine the corrosive result of that assumption on the church's view of its own angelology in the next chapter, but it is important to notice that the notion of a detached, observing "self" is a late Western cultural product. Other philosophies do not split reality into self and world, subject and object, as do we.

Religious and philosophical thought styles emerging from the Buddhist tradition, for example, emphasize the commonalities of self and world rather than their separation. Nichiren Shoshu Buddhist material, designed for American college students, argues that Buddhist gods represent the workings of a universal harmony. When a Nichiren Shoshu Buddhist prays, he does not pray to a god but fuses with a fundamental law of life in which both he and the god participate.

> The Law of the universe pervades all reality—both our lives and the environment. Buddhism maintains that first of all we must strive to shatter the illusion that we are somehow separate from our environment.... We are not entities unto ourselves; we exist in connection to the world around us.[4]

Philip and Jane, whose stories of angel encounters began this chapter, face skeptical, even hostile cultural and philosophical assumptions. I have attempted to identify at least the source from which some of that skepticism arises: a subject-object assumption that views angels as imaginary or as a psychological projection on the one hand, and "selves" who encounter an angel and who must explain that encounter with philosophical vocabularies that doom the attempt, on the other. In truth, once Philip and Jane accept subject-object formulations and use that vocabulary to describe their angel experiences, the more they might plead for understanding from our culture and from their church, the more strange and even freakish that experience sounds.

Philip and Jane know this, or they sense it. The more fervent their attempts to tell us how their angels came to them, what the angels said, and what the experiences meant, the more enmeshed in philosophical quandaries they seem to be. Their angel experiences occur in a culture where there is little intellectual room for such experiences except as supernatural events which are then summarily dismissed or otherwise devalued.

They know, too, that the ministry of a gracious God prompts them toward a gracious response. Philip wants to give to others some of what God has given him. Jane decided to abandon her path to the convent and seek an active life of service in helping others. It is noteworthy that each decision, touching on the religious meaning of a lifelong career and as consequential as any a person might make during a lifetime, is struggled through very privately with little or no help from the church. Philip tells no one about his angel experience except his wife and his brother and decides "to give back to others" in prayerful contemplation with God alone since, "the blessing of grace is its own belief." For her part, Jane decides to abandon a protected life, become involved with the opposite sex, finish her seminary education, and seek a career in the ministry. The spiritual motivation for these fateful decisions is shared with a few friends but with no church representative, be they rector or pastor.

There are large losses to be recounted here for Philip and Jane and for their church. Neither will experience a caring communal response to the most transforming spiritual experience of their adult lives. Neither is put in touch with the intellectual resources of their religious traditions regarding angels or with their impressive artistic expression. The church is deprived of precious testimony offering a glimpse of a larger universe whose God challenges priorities and settled ways and who changes the real lives of men and women in our own day. One need only remember the modest girl from a poor family whose life was changed forever by an angel named Gabriel. "The Holy Spirit will come upon you," he said, "and the power of the Most High will overshadow you; therefore the child to be born will be holy; he will be called Son of God."

There was a time, long ago, in a different world, where the reality of angels was never debated, where what angels said and did was a matter of life and death. I move back in history to acknowledge this other world, a more harmonious universe that did not make the assumptions that inform our modern culture or our contemporary church. It did not contemplate a "subject-object" philosophy. For hundreds of years, deep into the Middle Ages, the self had a reality in only one dimension: It belonged to God, whose angels ministered to that self and its faithful (or not so faithful) sojourn on this earth. We begin a theological and historical journey to pierce the mystery of how it came to be that the church, whose angelology played on center stage, came to that condition where angel appearances became an encounter best hidden from view.

## Notes

1. Abraham Maslow, *Religious Values and Peak Experiences* (Columbus, Ohio State University Press, 1964), 55.

2. I am indebted to Stephen Crite's "Angels We Have Heard," where this quotation was found. *Religion as Story*, ed. James B. Wiggins (New York, Harper & Row, 1978), 46.

3. Murray Stein, "The Dream of Wholeness," *Transformation* (Summer 1992): 12-13.

4. *Buddhism and Western Philosophical Tradition.* Publication of Soka Gakki International at the University of Maryland, College Park, 1992, 6.

# CHAPTER II

# Angels on Center Stage

Matthew, Mark, Luke, and John,
  Bless the bed that I lie on:
Four corners to my bed,
  Four angels round my head;
One to watch and one to pray,
  And two to bear my soul away.

This English nursery rhyme, written some three hundred years ago to comfort children at bedtime, introduces a time when angels were on center stage and assigned the most serious tasks: One angel watches and protects, one remains in constant prayer while the child sleeps, and, in an age when infant death was a tragic commonplace, two angels might take the child's soul to heaven and to God. Angels are guardians, they are in continuous worship and prayer, they bring souls to God, and, as we shall see, they also bring messages from God to men and women in their daily lives. In an age when Christian piety informed the bone and sinew of our entire Western civilization, what angels did was a matter of supreme, even ultimate concern, and their angel ministry a matter for theological comment and philosophical debate that endured for hundreds of years.

The thought that angels were *guardian* angels had already found theological expression in the writings of Philo Judaeus, the most important Jewish philosopher living at the time of Christ. Philo maintained that angels were employed by God in the exercise of his care over humankind. Angels are created, he said, "as servants of God for the performance of services of which our mortal race is in need."[1] Later, bit by bit, as a triumphant Christianity absorbed and digested the thought forms of a pagan world, the notion of angelic guardianship came to dominate the church's angelology so that more than one thousand years after Philo, Thomas Aquinas would bring this thought to its most powerful expression: God, he declared, appointed an individual guardian angel for every human being.

In the very beginning of the church's establishment, however, angels were viewed from many perspectives. They were seen as probation officers, physicians, social workers, judges, corporate executives, even mail carriers. In the process of its birth the Christian church faced a pagan Greco-Roman world saturated with popular notions about pre-existence. Are there structures or thoughts inside our heads before we are born? Do we have a soul, and if so, how did it arrive? According to a potent Christian tradition current during the second and third centuries, the answer was simple and clear. Yes, each human being had a soul before birth and that soul lived with God. While our bodies were being formed in the maternal womb, an angel sent from God delivered the soul into a suitable body much as a mailman might deliver a valuable package.[2]

The biblical scholar Origen, who died in A.D. 251 from wounds inflicted in the great Christian persecution by Emperor Decius, perhaps shared this conviction. He emphasized that our bodies are temporary environments for our souls. When the soul "falls" and is inserted into a body, that soul is then tested. Historical existence becomes a proving ground. The better the soul behaves, the more likely that it will ascend higher into pure soul existence. A disobedient soul, however, may fall lower after death into animal or plant life. Bodies that form environments for these souls must be as pure and wholesome as possible so that the souls might have their best opportunity. Thus, bodies living in this gross, fallen world, racked with passions and desires, must be disciplined and brought to true discipleship with Jesus.

God uses both demons and angels to accomplish this task, said Origen. The devil and his demons threaten men and women with illness and other forms of personal catastrophe when they live a life filled with bodily gratification or irrational desire. God has not driven the devil away from sovereignty over the world, so that these jolting threats might contribute to a restoration of a blessed state. Angels, on the other hand, lovingly guide and assist the soul in the course of its earthly life. If the soul has an evil thought, for example, angels minister to it. They may suggest that the evil thought was demon-influenced and then imbue the soul with the fortitude to resist that influence. However, if the soul should continue in an errant course, another order of angels specializing in judgments and penalties can be enlisted into the fray with their own brand of pastoral admonishments.

Less frequently, and for obdurately uncooperative sinners, there may need to be a bill of divorcement. In his commentary on the book of Deuteronomy, Origen says:

> A course may arise [in that the soul] does not find favor in the eyes of the angel who is her Lord and ruler because there is found an unseemly thing. A bill of divorcement [may] be written out so that the soul is no longer familiar with her familiar guardian and [the soul] is cast out.[3]

Origen can be even more explicit. In his commentary on Jeremiah, he suggests that there are those who are incurable even by another specialized group of angels, angel-physicians. These angels want to heal all those who have strayed, but some are not persuaded and must then be condemned as beyond all angelic help. Angels can mobilize an assortment of specialized pastoral powers to aid the souls of men and women through the dangerous vicissitudes of bodily life. They fight evil powers, they succor and sustain the soul in need, they provide power to replace bad thoughts by good ones, but they cannot force a virtuous lifestyle, and abandonment might finally, regrettably, be necessary.

By the beginning of the fifth century, Christianity had largely overcome its most ferocious political enemies and had seriously begun to convert the Greco-Roman world and bring it forth transformed and Christianized. So it was that the angelic specialization suggested by Origen was to be further elaborated and organized into a hierarchy of powers and values, as would be any serious enterprise within the Greco-Roman cultural world. This task was accomplished by a fifth-century theologian who wrote in Greek and who came to be known as Pseudo-Dionysius. "Pseudo" was appended to his name to distinguish him from Dionysius the Areopagite, mentioned in the seventeenth chapter of the book of Acts.

The organization of angels into a celestial hierarchy was truly a monumental undertaking, because Dionysius thought that angels should be organized in parallel with the hierarchy of clergy. Two of his great writings—*The Celestial Hierarchy*, which deals with angels, and *The Ecclesiastical Hierarchy*, dealing with bishops, had enormous influence within an expanding Christendom. Thomas Aquinas mentioned Pseudo-Dionysius in his own writings no less than 1,700 times.

Dionysius says that he writes about heavenly and earthly hierarchies to explain how each being, in proportion and order, is divinely perfected and how its powers are imparted to those below, according to their merit. Subordinates, in turn, should reach toward their superiors and thereby promote the advance of those below them. Thus, there is an inspired hierarchical harmony reaching upward toward those who are truly beautiful, wise, and good, and finally to God who is perfection itself.

There are nine angelic orders leading to the Divine core. The highest triad is made up of Seraphim, Cherubim, and Thrones. The second triad comprises Dominions, Virtues, and Powers. The third and lowest triad is composed of Principalities, Archangels, and Angels. The entire hierarchy vibrates, each element influencing the other in an upward and downward motion. The Divine revelation descends to its recipients and then uplifts them. Consider the first lines of *The Celestial Hierarchy*:

> Every good endowment and every perfect gift
> is from above, coming down from the Father
> of Lights. But there is something more.

> Inspired by the Father, each procession of the
> Light spreads itself generously toward us, and
> in its power to unify, it stirs us by lifting us up.
> It returns us back to the oneness and deifying
> simplicity of the Father who gathers us in.
> For, as the sacred Word says, "from him and
> to him are all things."[4]

"From him...and to him are all things." These words from the eleventh chapter of Paul's letter to the Romans lay the scriptural foundation for Dionysius's writings, but they also express the theme for one of the preeminent ideas by which European culture understood reality for a thousand years: a great chain of being, created by and emanating from God as the source of all being, and destined to be finally reassimilated by God in a back-and-forth movement forever.

The chords of this theme are struck repeatedly throughout the cultural efflorescence of a burgeoning European civilization. It is found everywhere—in literature, architecture, painting, music, the rituals of everyday life (even the banking system) in the church's liturgy and in its theology. Finally, it reaches a crescendo in the writing of Thomas Aquinas, canonized a saint by Pope John XXII in 1323 and declared Doctor of the Church by Pius V in 1567.

Born early in 1225 in his family's castle near Aquino in Italy, Thomas was entered by his parents as an oblate in the Benedictine monastery at Monte Cassino when he was five years old. In 1244 he decided to put aside his Benedictine habit to enroll in the Dominican order, where his intellectual prowess found expression in dazzling theological abilities. The thirteenth century called for the establishment of a universal Christian synthesis, which would receive all the truths the past had to teach. Thomas Aquinas set himself to this task in a monumental work, *Summa Theologica*, which was to be a grand exposition of Christian thought. Taking up the theological challenges of his own day, Aquinas spells out the distinction between natural reason and revelation and matches them as a couple. Human reason, such as that employed by any intelligent and educated person, can discover many things about God, including God's existence. Revelation, the Word of God in Scripture to which faith must give assent, makes up whatever shortfall reason leaves behind. The *Summa*, along with other writings identified as authoritative for the Catholic faithful, led to the ranking of Thomas Aquinas as probably the most prestigious and influential Catholic theologian of all time, even to this day.

At the Fourth Lateran Council in 1215, the church achieved a definitive formulation of the real presence of the body and blood of Christ in the Eucharist; this was called transubstantiation. That same Council also speculated extensively about the nature of angels, with a reaffirmation of the opening statements of the Nicene Creed, that God was the creator of all things visible and invisible, which meant both earthly and angelic creatures. A new exposition of Catholic thought must then include a clear, precise, and detailed discussion of the celestial beings that God had created. St. Thomas responded with the most detailed and substantial explanation of angels undertaken since Pseudo-Dionysius, some eight hundred years earlier, and until the Protestant theologian, Karl Barth, almost seven hundred years later.

The *Summa Theologica* is an exceedingly difficult and tiresome book for the contemporary mind. It is written in medieval scholastic style and proceeds to unfold its meanings in an unvarying ritual of question, proposition, objection, and reply. The section on angels includes fourteen questions, each of which is further subdivided into others. For example, the first section under Angels is labeled "The Substance of the Angels Absolutely Considered." It then proceeds to ask various questions, such as: Is an angel altogether incorporeal? Is an angel composed of matter and form? Do angels exist in any great numbers?

Under each of these questions, the *Summa* lists objections, many of which were posed by theologians and philosophers who had written about angels perhaps many hundreds of years before. In Objection No.1, the *Summa* has John of Damascus, an eighth-century scholar and theologian, say, "An angel is said to be incorporeal and immaterial as regards us; but compared to God, he is corporeal and material." To each objection, St. Thomas makes a reply in carefully measured sentences. To Objection No.1 his reply is:

> Incorporeal substances rank between God and corporeal creatures. Now the medium compared to one extreme appears to be the other extreme, as what tepid compared to heat seems to be cold; and thus it is said that angels compared to God are material and corporeal, not, however, as if anything corporeal existed in them.[5]

The entire treatise is written in this strange, stylized fashion, common and expected in serious theological or philosophical discourse in the thirteenth century, a method designed for perfect intellectual precision and lucidity very much like mathematical equations.

St. Thomas begins his discussion of angels where Pseudo-Dionysius began his: a metaphysical speculation on the hierarchical grades of being. Different kinds of being are arranged in an order of increasing or decreasing value: minerals, vegetables, animals, and then human beings. It is a ladder, as it were, leading higher and higher in the Spirit toward God. But if these were the only creatures on the ladder, the general plan of creation would reveal an obvious gap. The hierarchy of being must be seamless and continuous; therefore, angels are required to fill up the spaces between God and human beings. Hence, St. Thomas begins the treatise with the first article and the first question, asking whether an angel is altogether incorporeal. He answers with the assertion that there must be some incorporeal creatures, because the perfection of the universe demands it. There must be creatures of an incorporeal nature to fill up the space between the sovereign simplicity of God and the complexity of material bodies, and we call these creatures angels. Angels are a reality on two grounds: They are spoken of in Scripture, and they are a theological necessity. Moreover, they are at the top of the ladder in order to state the final superiority of grace over nature and revelation over reason.

Further following the schema of Pseudo-Dionysius, St. Thomas grades and classifies different orders of angels from the first to the last. The first order of angels is known as the Seraphim and Cherubim, aglow with love for God, whom they know with a perfect love. They "sojourn in the vestibule of divinity" and are entrusted with the secrets of God's governance. A second order, the Dominions, controls the ministry of divine power. The Dominions have authority to prescribe what other angels must carry out, issuing directives that the angels beneath them multiply and channel according to the various effects that are desired. The third class of angels, the order of Providence, is placed in immediate charge of the administration of things human. Some of these angels are concerned with the common good and general welfare of nations and cities. The distinction of kingdoms, the transference of temporary supremacy of one nation rather than another, and the leadership of royalty and other great men and women belong to their administration.

At the bottom of this general order, are angels whose effects have to do with individual persons in their day-to-day lives. These are guardian angels, who are sent as God's ministers and messengers for important announcements. On this subject the *Summa* includes an entire section, "The Guardianship of the Good Angels," which falls under the title of "The Divine Government." In this, St. Thomas places the effective interaction of angels with the affairs of human beings within the issue of governance, particularly in regard to God's providence.

St. Thomas takes pains to explain that God does not abandon his creatures and provides guardian angels to help. Human beings on their own and by themselves are prone to instability. Under pressure from their unruly inclinations, they are in danger of error, sometimes serious and fateful error, so God sends angels to induce in humankind tendencies to do what is right and good. Even the most grievous sinners have faithful and kindly friends whose assistance is unfailing.

To the proposition that all human beings have individual guardian angels assigned to them, St. Thomas answers two objections. It is true, he says, that one human being can have guardianship over many other human beings; however, it is in the nature of God's providence that each individual person, the bearer of a portion of the Spirit, has a particular angel who presides over him or her. Second, although men and women are equal in nature, still inequality exists. Some of this inequality is caused by the fact that God has diversified their ways and placed some, rather than others, in positions of great exaltation and authority, but some inequality is also the result of sin, which God has cursed, bringing the sinner low. It would not be rational to believe that one angel might exercise an effective guardianship over such a diverse group, some high and some low for a variety of reasons; therefore, each person is guarded by one angel. The guardian angel is believed to be a good friend who will render the most humble service to fit our needs, even in small matters.

A section is devoted to the question of whether angels are appointed to guard all human beings, including heathens and unbelievers. St. Thomas begins this discourse with the thought that in this life we are all on a road by which we should journey toward heaven. On this road we are threatened by many dangers, both within and without. The providential nature of God decrees that all human beings should have guardians, because, as wayfarers, they must pass along unsafe roads. Heathens are not guaranteed an eternal life in heaven even by their good works, but they are protected from certain evils by a good guardian angel given to them by an act of divine providence.

Is a guardian angel appointed to us from the moment of birth? St. Thomas recognizes two differing opinions: One claims that an angel is appointed at baptism because we receive the inheritance of salvation at that time; this is a most appropriate occasion at which to receive the ministry of one's guardian angel. St. Thomas adopts the other position: Although it may be that a guardian is not assigned before birth, one is appointed at the very moment of birth. He says:

> As long as the child is in the mother's womb,
> it is not entirely separate, but by reason of a
> certain intimate tie it is still part of her; just as

the fruit while hanging on the tree is part of
the tree. And, therefore, it can be said, with
some degree of probability, that the angel who
guards the mother guards the child while in
the womb. But, when the child becomes separate from the mother at birth, an angel
guardian is appointed to it, as St. Jerome says.[6]

In response to the issue of whether guardian angels ever
forsake us, St. Thomas maintains that neither human beings
nor anything else can be entirely withdrawn from the providence of God. On the other hand, sometimes God does not
protect us from trouble, or even from falling into sin, and we
will then suffer some punishment. The guardian angel is not
forsaking us by allowing these particular misfortunes because:

> Although an angel may forsake a person some-
> times locally, he does not for that reason for-
> sake him as to the effect of his guardianship,
> for even when he is in heaven he knows what
> is happening to each person; nor does [the
> angel] need time for his locomotion, for he
> can be with us in an instant.[7]

I cannot leave the angelology of St. Thomas without point-
ing out his belief that not all spiritual beings are good or good
for us. Angels can sin, and some of them did. St. Thomas says
that sinning angels are prone to the sins of pride and envy, and
their evil is compounded because they then lead men and
women into every other kind of sinful disobedience against
God. Lucifer, called Satan, and his sinning angels or demons,
are obstinate and inflexible in their ceaseless battle against
human salvation and are determined to lead human beings
into hell, where they will witness the punishment of the
damned, tormented by fire and other awful afflictions.

Lucifer, leader of the fallen angels, began his rebellion in
heaven because of his prideful desire to be as God. He did not
sin at the very moment of his creation, but immediately afterward. He rejected the grace into which he had been created and

wanted to be like God in a way not intended by nature—for example, by creating things through his own power, or achieving final beatitude without God's help, or having command over others in a way proper to God alone.

In a later development it was thought that Lucifer, or Satan, might invade our hearts and inhabit our souls so as to obliterate yearnings for goodness and for God's grace. These invaders were called incubus and succubus, devils who cunningly induced their victims into a variety of evils. They were most adept at incubating sexual sins, including the impregnation of chosen women whose issue would most certainly become a witch. The identification of incubus and succubus devils was one of the central issues that occupied the church's pastoral ministry during the Middle Ages, when the pastoral office devoted itself to "discerning the spirits" that might inhabit sinful and sick souls. Elaborate manuals were written to help pastors and confessors identify whether the spirit who occupied our deepest personal interiors was, for example, a devil, or it was hoped, a good spirit—an angel.[8] Strange as it may seem to modern men and women, examples of demon possession and the practice of exorcism can be cited in every epoch of Christian history, especially in the Catholic tradition. Protestants have, by and large, taken a skeptical attitude, and whenever the Protestant ethos was dominant, exorcism was rarely used.

The angelology of Thomas Aquinas is, undoubtedly, a prodigious achievement, unmatched in Western culture before or since. It has an overwhelming aesthetic appeal. The great ladder of being starts with the highest degree of perfection, realized by God, and descends in minute steps downward through human beings to minerals and rocks, whose very existence, their being, testifies to the glory of God. For medieval minds steeped in the sciences of their day, this magnificent schema not only was believable, but was a philosophical home for all things in heaven and on earth. It reflects a unity of all creation, as well as connections between the past, the creation of the universe, the present being born, and the future—foretold and certain—unfolding according to God's plan.

Delight in the beauty, the proportion, and the fullness of St. Thomas's understanding of angels is not the only chord of appreciation we men and women of today can sound for his angelology. We are in his debt, as well, for his theological precision. St. Thomas's discussion of angels is placed carefully under the doctrine of providence. Angels are ministers of God's *providence*, not God's redemption, whose minister can be only Jesus Christ. Placement under providence also implies that God's angels help and assist all human beings, those who have never heard of Jesus Christ, as well as all believers and unbelievers alike. Angels do good and help human beings everywhere, even when not recognized or identified as God's agents and messengers.

He is insistent that each person, one by one, is identified, known in heaven, and assigned a special spiritual being who fights on our side and wishes only the most noble and most virtuous for us, and who works and prays continuously for our health and well-being. Each human being *without exception*, declares St. Thomas, has a guardian angel during his or her entire earthly life, a spiritual companion who will never abandon us.

Finally, St. Thomas warns us that simply because something is very good does not mean it cannot be also very evil. There are bad spiritual beings abroad in this world. As St. Thomas never doubted the reality of God's angels, so he believed in malevolent demons, whose destructive power was independent of our own. They were always there, ever ready to sabotage God's plans for health and salvation. St. Thomas's unromantic assessment of this world and the precariousness of our human condition is a useful warning to the popular angelologies making their way underground in our culture today.

Yet, appreciative as we may be, we cannot contort our thinking into the mindset of the thirteenth century. That mind was, in significant measure, based on scientific assumptions we have long since discarded. Almost everyone in the thirteenth century, perhaps also Thomas Aquinas, believed that the earth was flat and attached by colossal hooks to a revolving heaven where God and the angels held court. Beginning in the sixteenth century, a new astronomy demolished the idea of the earth as the center of the universe and of a heaven above whose main concern was earth's own ultimate welfare. If the earth is one planet among many, which revolves around the sun rather than vice versa, and heaven is not above nor hell below, then where is God and where are angels?

The world that Thomas Aquinas inherited, and to which he bequeathed his stupendous theological edifice, suffered another enormous shock in the years following. The horrified population of Europe faced the scourge of the Black Death, losing more than one quarter of its population. As Europe lay in its agony, the church and its saints, with its legions of angels, tried to combat the menace but could not turn it back. Angels could not escape the intimation of emptiness and impotence that experience impressed into the minds of the people everywhere in Europe.

Under the merciless pressure of the Black Death and the findings of a new kind of astronomy, the elaborate hierarchies of the angelic hosts came to be questioned and then, reluctantly, bit by bit, abandoned. The once teeming metropolis that was the heavenly city slowly emptied, and the worldview that had constructed it lay tattered, its energy seeping away.

The emerging discoveries of science and a new readiness to question past certainties demanded fresh thinking and a supporting philosophy to embrace new realities. The intellectual dynamism that incarnated that emerging spirit came in the person of René Descartes, possibly the greatest of all French philosophers and certainly one of the most influential. Descartes was born on March 31, 1596, in La Haye, France, of parents who belonged to the lesser nobility. The youngest of three children, he enjoyed an income from property he inherited from his mother sufficient to make him independent throughout his life. He died in Sweden, where he had gone at the invitation of Queen Christina, who wished to be instructed in his philosophy.

In 1637, Descartes published his first philosophical treatise, *Discourse on the Method of Rightly Conducting Reason and Seeking for Truth in the Sciences*. In it, Descartes unfolds his fundamental aim: to attain philosophical truth by the use of reason. "I wished to give myself entirely to the search after truth,"⁹ he said. But what he was seeking was not a multiplicity of isolated truths; rather, it was a system of propositions in which nothing would be assumed except for that which was self-evident and indisputable.

When it was possible to do so, Descartes avoided discussion of theological matters. He was, he said, a philosopher and mathematician and not a theologian, and he would, therefore, pursue his philosophical concerns on the side of reason alone. He had accepted, without question, St. Thomas's proposition that reason enabled one to discover many truths, including God's existence, and he offered his own proofs of God's existence which he claimed to be absolutely valid for all time. In agreement with St. Thomas, he recognized there were other truths that were revealed by God and appropriated by faith. Angels came into this category, and although their existence was beyond human comprehension, they were, nonetheless, a reality. Descartes declared himself to be a faithful and believing Catholic to his last day.

Seeking to discover an indubitable truth by reason, Descartes came to the now-famous affirmation, *cogito ergo sum*, I think, therefore I am. However much I doubt, I must exist; otherwise I could not doubt. I may be deceived by believing that what I perceive about the material world is true, or even deceived in thinking that the propositions of mathematics or geometry are certainly true; but however I extend the application of doubt, I cannot doubt my own existence. *Cogito ergo sum* was to be the foundation for Descartes's philosophy. It was a fateful decision, one that altered the entire course of Western philosophy. If "I think, therefore I am," what then is the character of the "I" who does the thinking? Descartes concludes that the "I" is a distinct and separate substance, different from everything else on the face of the earth, including one's own body. There is nothing corporeal in the substance of the thinking mind. It is pure, entirely spirit, a point of clear essence from which to view the world. Outside our minds, "out there," what we observe are either inanimate objects like rocks and minerals, or vegetation, or machines like our bodies or those of animals. There are spiritual substances—the mind, for example—and there are material substances which have length, depth, breadth, and weight. The material world is a world of matter with geometrical extension and motion. The thinking world is different. It is the essence of self, for the "I", said Descartes, was himself. "I," he said, "am a thing which thinks."[10]

In his view, there is no intrinsic relationship between one's mind, which Descartes often called the soul, and one's body. The mind relates to the body as a mover to the moved or a driver to a machine. Indeed, the body is a machine as animals are machines. They have no minds, they cannot think, they are nothing but matter in motion. The mind, or soul, drives the body as a captain might steer a ship. How the mind would do so was, of course, a difficult problem. Descartes said that a gland, the pineal gland, received instructions from the mind; these directives were then transmitted as "animal spirits" by means of the "minute canals of the body's fibers" into the body machine, which produced the movements and sensations we experience.

Descartes had addressed the medieval unity of body and spirit and separated it into mind and matter. The old belief that animals, and even vegetation, are sensitive to the spirit and participate in the great ladder of being leading to God, was shattered. Bodies and animals are not sacred; they are merely meat, matter in motion to be dissected, weighed, classified, and, of course, used. Thus, Descartes brings the idea of a "subject-object" world to life and so begins the long schism between science and religion and the birth of modern philosophy.

In his book *Earth in the Balance*, Vice President Albert Gore is moved to observe that this split between mind and body, spirit and matter, carried the profound implication that a new power, scientific knowledge, could be used to dominate nature with moral impunity.

> This fundamental shift in Western thinking—
> which in a very real sense marks the beginning
> of modern history—gave humankind increasing
> dominance in the world, as a flood of scientific

discoveries began unlocking the secrets of God's blueprint for the universe. But how could this new power be used wisely? Descartes [...] ensured the gradual abandonment of the philosophy that humankind is one vibrant strand in an elaborate web of life, matter and meaning.[11]

The subject-object thought forms bequeathed to us by René Descartes did not banish angels but relentlessly marginalized them into the realm of the supernatural, as decorative objects or psychological projections. When science advanced, the ancient idea of spiritual "realities" retreated and angels were intellectually doomed as "not real."

Neither Philip nor Jane needs to know of René Descartes or to have read one page of his philosophy, but they had, in fact, inherited the thought world he created. They found themselves unable to think in any other terms or to explain themselves to any audience that could understand their angel encounters in any other formulation. In truth, once they accept these subject-object formulations and use that vocabulary to describe their experiences, the attempt loses intellectual credibility and becomes "religious" and, therefore, scientifically disreputable.

The subject-object world that had caught Philip and Jane so completely, so inexorably, was not given by God; it was, rather, the philosophical invention of a genius whose ideas have dominated for centuries and are powerful to this day. However, Descartes's subject-object world is being questioned by new thinkers who are making it possible to return to a kind of spiritual unity we have not experienced for four hundred years, reviving the possibility of viewing angels other than as "objects" to be tested and then dismissed by the canons of scientific method.[12]

But before I proceed further, I must turn back in time some one hundred years before René Descartes to the Protestant Reformation and those thinkers and theologians who broke away from the established church. We will consider how their theology deliberated upon the heavenly hosts and how angels fared in their vocabulary of faith.

*Notes*

1. Quoted in Henry A. Wolfson, *Philo Foundations of Religious Philosophy in Judaism, Christianity and Islam* (Cambridge, MA: Harvard University Press, 1948), 372.

2. See Henri Crouzel, *Origen*, trans. A. S. Worrall (Edinburgh: T & T Clarke, 1989), 205ff.

3. John Clark Smith, *The Ancient Wisdom of Origen* (Lewisburg, PA: Bucknell University Press, 1992), 89.

4. *Pseudo-Dionysius: The Complete Works*, trans. Colm Luibheid (New York: Paulist Press, 1987), 145.

5. *St. Thomas Aquinas: Basic Writings,* Vol. I, edited and annotated with an introduction by Anton C. Pegis (New York: Random House, 1944), 1043.

6. Ibid., 1044.

7. Ibid., 1047.

8. See William Clebsch and Charles Jaekle, *Pastoral Care in Historical Perspective* (Northvale, New Jersey and London: Jason Aronson,Inc., The Masterwork Series, 1994), 190-202.

9. René Descartes, *Discourse on the Method of Rightly Conducting Reason and Seeking for Truth in the Sciences, Great Books of the Western World*, trans. Elizabeth S. Holdane and G. R. T. Ross (Chicago: The University of Chicago Press: 1952), 9.

10. See Frederick Copleston, S.J., *A History of Philosophy,* vol. 4, *Descartes to Leibnitz* (London: Burns, Oates & Washbourne, 1958).

11. Albert Gore, *Earth in the Balance* (Boston, New York, London: Houghton-Mifflin, 1992), 252-253.

12. See Albert Borgmann, *Crossing the Postmodern Divide* (Chicago: University of Chicago Press, 1992), and Charles Taylor, *Sources of the Self* (Cambridge, MA: Harvard University Press, 1989).

# CHAPTER III

# Angels Offstage

Reacting against a medieval church it believed had absorbed too much of a pagan world, Reformation Protestantism set out to cleanse its own house. It banished the saints and the Virgin Mary, and angels disappeared from view. The Protestant mind was, finally, depopulated.

This did not happen all at once, and it happened in its most unqualified form in American Protestantism. As Philip and Jane face their churches, they find dull indifference or a stubborn skepticism toward angels and their encounters with them. How and why this state of affairs developed within the American religious establishment is a fascinating story.

Martin Luther (1483-1546) took up the subject of angels in ten sermons preached during his lifetime. According to Bengt Hoffman, an internationally acclaimed Luther scholar, not one of these sermons was included in any English language edition of Luther's writings. Hoffman thinks a particular theological mindset determined the omission. Angels, it seems, were considered to be part of a primitive medieval lore best left unpublished. In addition, Protestant consciousness found it difficult to accept Luther's notion—in agreement with Thomas Aquinas—that demons or dark angels are a constant reality with which the human condition must contend.

Luther begins with a vision of the entire creation as being involved in a colossal battle. Individuals and the church are engaged in that struggle waged on this earth and carried on in realms far beyond the visible world. Luther's hymn, *Ein Feste Burg*, puts our human situation in focus:

A mighty fortress is our God,
   A bulwark never failing;

For still our ancient foe
Doth seek to work us woe;
His craft and power are great,
And, armed with cruel hate,
On earth is not his equal.

And though this world, with devils filled,
   Should threaten to undo us;
We will not fear, for God hath willed
   His truth to triumph through us;

The prince of darkness grim,
We tremble not for him;
His rage we can endure,
For lo! His doom is sure,
One little word shall fell him.

We, here on earth caught between dark angels and good angels, reflect the cosmic struggle between the devil and Christ.

A Christian should know that he is sitting among devils and that the devil is closer to him than his coat and his shirt, yes, closer than his own skin; indeed he is all around us, that we are always at loggerheads with him...Remember and be watchful...do not allow yourselves to believe he is far away. No, he is your foe—and not just your foe in general. He is actively evil and [with all his angels]...fired by unspeakable fury, aims to devour you.[1]

"But," says Luther, "although there are many demons, we must know that good angels abound. They defend, and keep us."

> Thus each ruler, citizen, householder, each Christian has his angel who takes care of him.... As when someone is about to drown in deep water and I am at that place and pull him up, thereby saving his life, in a similar fashion the good angels deal with someone in danger; they speak to his heart, they turn him around, saying, "This you must not do," and so forth. Thus they protect us.... Hence we have the saying—and that indeed is well said, "You had a good angel today. "[2]

That Martin Luther, intellectual and spiritual leader of the Reformation, should espouse an angelology so closely identified with Thomas Aquinas is arresting. That it also includes enthusiasm for the ministry of guardian angels is surprising.

With one exception, Emanuel Swedenborg, the Protestant reformers who followed Luther did not find his fascination with angels necessary for their own theological formulations. John Calvin (1509-1564), the most systematic of the early reformers, had an angelology which, unlike Luther's, was largely cautionary or negative. He had concluded that most of what had been taught about angels through the ages had been arrogant speculation. He declared that speculative theologians like Pseudo-Dionysius and Thomas Aquinas prattled on about angels in dangerous ways. Calvin emphasized the limits of discussion about angels, because, he concluded, what we deal with are unfathomable mysteries, not appropriate for human beings to discuss except in accordance with strict scriptural authority.

John Wesley, the spiritual founder of the Methodist Church, was more than mildly interested in angels. His sermons, hymns, and his Journal reflect a curiosity about them far surpassing that of John Calvin. Born in 1703, one of fifteen children, Wesley was educated at Oxford and ordained a priest in the Church of England in 1728. He was a notably vigorous man with so much energy he confessed that he did not begin to feel old until he was eighty-five. He was a tireless writer and preacher, traveled everywhere in England and

Scotland, and visited the United States. From the age of thirty-six, he logged 225,000 miles as he preached forty thousand sermons to tens of thousands of men, women, and children at a time.

John Wesley found it necessary to begin his discussion of angels by decrying the evils and excesses of the Roman Catholics. He said that angels, along with Mary and the saints, were objects of worship by the "Church of Rome," and, as proof, he quoted the *Children's Catechism* published in 1678 by the Catholic Archdiocese of London. Wesley said the *Catechism* made it clear:

> The Church of Rome teaches that angels are to be worshiped, invoked, and prayed to. And they have litanies and prayers composed for this purpose. They teach that as every particular person hath a guardian angel from his birth, so it is fit to commit themselves more particularly to [their angels] after this manner: "Blessed angel! To whose care our loving Creator hath committed me, defend me this day, I beseech you, from all dangers and direct me in the way I ought to walk."[3]

Wesley took pains to point out that only God is to be worshiped, as Scripture commands in Matthew 4:10:

> Jesus said to him, "Away with you, Satan! For it is written, 'Worship your God, and serve only him.'"

He said that the faithful are to honor the holy angels, as they are

> sent forth to minister unto them that shall be heirs of salvation, but not to worship or pray to them; we dare not, as it is what they themselves refuse and abhor, and the Scripture doth condemn as a sign of a fleshly mind vain-

ly intruding into those things which we have
not seen.[4]

The cautionary ambivalence of this quotation is to be noted.
It is an almost perfect expression of the temperament that
informed the Protestantism that came to the American
colonies and that later expanded on their frontier. It is a quotation that could easily be assented to by Increase Mather
(1639-1723), the Calvinistic New England divine, or Jonathan
Edwards (1703-1758), American Congregational theologian,
and by scores of clergy, the educated and not so educated, as
well as the itinerant field and stump preachers who fascinated
frontier folk in a rapidly expanding America.

With the exception of Martin Luther and Swedenborg
whom I will discuss later in this chapter, the Protestant ethos,
European and American, began with limiting statements, saying that angels ought not be seen as having any standing of
their own as objects of worship, and we ought not indulge in
Catholic-like speculations about them. After this *bona fides*,
most reformers expressed other dimensions of their ambivalence, including assertions that seem, on the surface, to be in
contradiction to their own warnings. John Wesley not only
believed angels existed, but he celebrated their sustaining and
protective abilities as well. In one of his later sermons, he
includes a poem from the pen of Bishop Ken,

> O may thy angels while I sleep,
> Around my bed their vigils keep;
> Their love angelical instill,
> Stop every avenue of ill!
> May they celestial joys rehearse,
> And thought to thought with me converse!

Ken adds the ancient prayer for Saint Michael's and All
Angels' Day used by the Church of England in his own day.

> O everlasting God, who hast ordained and con-
> stituted the services of angels and men in a
> wonderful manner; grant as thy holy angels

always do Thee service in heaven so by thy
appointment they may succor and defend us
on earth, through Jesus Christ our Lord.[5]

Wesley was also curious about the varieties of angelic phenomena. He knew, he said, only three people who claimed to
have direct intercourse with the Godhead; but supernatural
visions, communion with spirits, and sensing angelic presence
had always aroused his interest, though he wanted to conduct
his own investigation of the evidence.

Margaret Barlow, a servant girl, said she had seen a beautiful angel, clothed in white, "glistening like silver" with
speech "unspeakably musical," who foretold certain events
which she attested to be true. Wesley wrote that he "asked her
an abundance of questions, and...was soon convinced that she
was not only sincere, but deep in grace, and therefore incapable of deceit." The only slight difficulty with the account,
according to Wesley, was that the young woman always
referred to her angel as female, whereas Scripture, he said,
unquestionably made angels male. Yet, explains Wesley, from
the face, the voice, and the apparel, one might easily mistake
him for female, but this mistake was of little consequence.

Charles Wesley, John's older brother, was the author of
more than six thousand poems, many of which were set to
music as hymns. Dozens of them had to do with angels and
personal encounters with them. In the hymn, "Come O
Thou Traveler Unknown," referring to Jacob's wrestling
with the strange angel-like creature on the banks of the
Jabbok, the faithful sing:

Come O thou Traveler unknown,
    Whom still I hold, but cannot see;
My company before is gone,
    and I am left alone with thee,
With thee all night I mean to stay
    And wrestle till the break of day.

The current hymnal of the Episcopal Church includes this
hymn and five others written by Charles Wesley featuring

angels and their ministry.

I will return again to discuss John Wesley's conversion experience as a further indication of how his religious life, the content and style of his theology, and his ambivalence about angels reflected to a remarkable degree the tone of much American religious experience. But I turn now to examine the angelology of Wesley's contemporary whose religious thought deviated markedly from the prevailing theological inclination. Emanuel Swedenborg (1688-1772) was the son of a professor of theology and Lutheran bishop who was himself a scientist, philosopher, and prolific writer on spiritual subjects. Swedenborg was a distinguished thinker, showing remarkable originality on a number of subjects. He anticipated many later hypotheses on magnetics and nebular theories about the formation of the sun and planets. He is generally regarded as the father of modern crystallography. In 1714 he was appointed to the Swedish Board of Mines, from which he resigned three years later to give his life to the study of spiritual phenomena, including his experiences with angels. He was never ordained in the Lutheran Church, and while he resisted founding a religious sect, his followers formed themselves into a society called "The Church of the New Jerusalem," or simply, "The New Church."

Swedenborg was single-minded and enthusiastic about angels, rather than cautionary and ambivalent as were most of his Protestant brethren. According to Swedenborg, angels are numerous and everywhere. They are realities far superior to humankind and the bearers of God's wisdom to men and women in everyday life. Angels breathe and speak with vowels and consonants. Swedenborg reported an angelic encounter in which,

> [when] a certain angel who had been known to me appeared and spoke with his lips, which when I mentioned it to him...that angels have no lips and consequently he could not speak with them, he nevertheless persisted and taught a lively demonstration.[7]

Swedenborg said he experienced many conversations with angels, some simply as friend-to-friend and others of a more formal nature, but all of them were edifying and intending praise and glory to God.

Angels also write, he said. They do so by controlling a "medium" or the medium's hand. Swedenborg did much of such automatic writing, which he attributed to angelic influence. He could exclaim that his hand moved of itself, writing things that were "arcana"—secrets never known to anyone before. He took much of what he wrote of biblical commentary as revelation from God that came to him in this special way.

Inhabited by angels, not only was Swedenborg's world a curiosity, but the nonchalance with which he discussed angels brought him, and later the Swedenborgians, under suspicion that both he and they suffered from mental illness. William James (1842-1910), noted American psychologist and philosopher, himself the son of a Swedenborgian clergyman, thought it necessary to comment on Emanuel Swedenborg's sanity. He concluded that although he might never be able to believe in or even understand Swedenborg's spiritual world, one had to fight against the tendency to classify religious impulses, however strange, as pathology. He thought it better to avoid psychological speculation about how religious expression came about and to concentrate on its significance and value once it is here.

That Swedenborg and the Swedenborgians expressed a religiosity of a different sort, James had no doubt. But their differences, expressed in the New Jerusalem Church, now migrated to the United States are illustrative of a central concern of this book: how it came to be that angels disappeared from ecclesiastical view. And disappear is what they most certainly did.

In the winter of 1914-1915, the King's Chapel Lectures were delivered under the auspices of the Lowell Institute in King's Chapel, Boston. These lectures were published by the Harvard University Press in 1917. William Worchester, president and professor of Scriptural Interpretation and Homiletics at the New Church Theological School in

Cambridge, delivered the lecture on the Swedenborgians. His lecture can be timed at approximately thirty-five minutes, during which Mr. Worchester touched on the basic doctrines of the New Jerusalem Church and devoted the rest of his talk to its development since establishment in Boston in 1818. Only once in the entire lecture did the word "angel" appear, and that in a passing reference to how Swedenborg's association with angels illuminated his scriptural interpretations.[8] Angels, it seems, were vanishing from the public expression of Swedenborgian religion. Their departure was neither noticed nor mourned. Angels had faded away.

The New Jerusalem Church, though the most noticeable, was not the only ecclesiastical group to have pushed angels out of mind and into whatever intellectual back alley was available. By the middle of the nineteenth century, everywhere in American religious life and in most non-Catholic faith groups, angels languished and, finally homeless, they disappeared.

I can offer at least three explanations of why and how angels came to be an endangered species, both in American ecclesiastical consciousness and in its intellectual expression. First, it must be noted that non-Catholic religious thought, Martin Luther and the Swedenborgians excepted, never developed an angelology that was central to its theological concern. Protestant angelology spoke in a soft voice and began its speech with warnings and limits. Until Karl Barth, angels were almost forgotten. Of all the Protestant reformers (again, Luther and Emanuel Swedenborg excepted), John Wesley was the most interested and curious about angels, but he never lost his ambivalence about them and they never occupied as lively a theological position as they did for Luther and, later, Swedenborg.

Second, since the advent of René Descartes and the beginnings of modern philosophy and science, the intellectual climate for angels turned dangerous. Not only could angels not survive the fact that the earth was a very minor planet circling a mediocre star, neither could they survive a subject-object world in which they were banished into a crass supernaturalism. Indeed, the entire theological enterprise fought for its life along an extended front against the powerful forces of secularism, a burgeoning science, and newly emerging philosophies offering no comfort to religion in any of its forms. Angels were a small platoon along that front, an intellectual embarrassment; they could easily be abandoned when retreat was strategic and urgent.

Third, and possibly most important, angels are mediating creatures; they are ambassadors from God. American religion, however, is experiential and immediate. Americans do not need or want an intermediary between themselves and God. Their religious consciousness is personal, datable, one-on-one. It is a style born from religious conversion experiences, which stands at the heart of American evangelical religion.

Consider the conversion of John Wesley himself as a paradigm for that experience. His conversion took place on May 24, 1738, at 8:45 P.M. He says,

> In the evening I went very unwillingly to a society [meeting] in Aldersgate-Street, where [a man] was reading Luther's preface to the Epistle to the Romans. About a quarter to nine, while he was describing the change which God works in the heart through faith in Christ, I felt myself strangely warmed. I felt I did trust in Christ, Christ alone for salvation: And an assurance was given me, that he had taken away my sins, even mine, and saved me from the law of sin and death.[9]

Conversion is an emotional experience. In order to be a Christian, as opposed to an almost-Christian, one must feel that one's sins are forgiven and be able to say when and under what circumstances that event occurred.[10] What seems so mild, even genteel here in Wesley, became fierce, even raging in the enthusiasms of American religion, especially in its Southern Baptist and Pentecostal forms. What need, then, for the mediating function of angels and the heavenly hosts? One was converted and knew he or she was saved from sin and death by the blood of the Lamb. Compared with this, all other knowledge and all other messages paled into insignificance.

Angels were never a large presence in the American religious experience; and as that experience became more and more institutionalized, their appearance, muted to begin with, faded from view. But angels were not extinguished; quietly, without notice or regret, they moved into a spiritual underground detached from official theological interest. There, in a myriad of cultural expressions, some touching and beautiful, others bizarre and even pathological, they took hold in the spiritual longing of millions.

The indifference, annoyance, and perhaps hostility, with which most Protestant congregations might greet the angel encounters reported by Philip and Jane have a long history in the American religious consciousness. Yet, outside official ecclesiastical concern and in the realm of individual and private spiritual experience, angels appear, delivering messages of care and hope. But before I discuss theological and pastoral bridges that might lead American churches to a more welcoming environment for Christian believers who have experienced an angel visitation, I turn to the thought of two modern and very different religious thinkers: Karl Barth and Carl Jung. Each had much to say about angels but, like Philip and Jane, discovered that their interest in that subject was met with less than enthusiasm by their contemporaries and those who followed them. Karl Barth devoted a significant portion of his *Church Dogmatics* to angelology, yet it is the most neglected of his entire theological corpus. The *Collected Works* of Carl Jung lists more than one hundred references to angels, yet one seeks in vain for Jung's thoughts on that subject in any popular compendium of his writings. Nonetheless, what both Barth and Jung have to say about angels is of central importance to our discussion, for each of them, and from his own quite different discipline, has issued a warning that we do well to heed.

## Notes

1. *On the Angels: A Sermon by Martin Luther of 1530*, translated with comments by Bengt Hoffman (Printed by GAM, Gettysburg, PA 1985).

2. Ibid., 1.

3. Charles W. Carter, ed., *A Contemporary Wesleyan Theology* (Grand Rapids, MI: Francis Asbury Press, 1983), Wesley's remarks on the Roman Catechism, 1059.

4. Ibid., 1061.

5. Stanley Ayling, *John Wesley* (Nashville, TN: Abingdon Press, 1979), 301.

6. Ibid., 302.

7. Signe Toksvig, *Emanuel Swedenborg: Scientist and Mystic* (New Haven, CT: Yale University Press, 1948), 264.

8. *The Religious History of New England: King's Chapel Lectures* (Cambridge, MA: Harvard University Press, 1917), 332.

9. *The Journal of John Wesley*, edited with an introduction by Elizabeth Jay (New York: Oxford University Press, 1987), 34-35.

10. See R.A. Knox, *Enthusiasm: A Chapter in the History of Religion* (New York: Oxford University Press, 1950), 538 ff.; and Harold Bloom, *The American Religion* (New York: Simon and Schuster, 1991), 18-49.

# CHAPTER IV

# Beware:
# Homeless Angels

A centerpiece of popular piety in American religious life is the conviction that every person can attain his or her own relationship to God, with the majority firmly believing that God loves them individually, within or without the church. According to an article published in *The Washington Post*, that belief is reflected in a folk angelology. It included the report that 76 percent of five hundred teenagers polled believe in guardian angels, a percentage that has been increasing since 1978, when 64 percent believed in angels. The pollster also reported that less than half of these same adolescents went to church regularly or could identify the person who delivered the Sermon on the Mount. One "angelologist" in Santa Cruz, California, called for a Get-to-Know-Your-Guardian-Angel-Day, which she hoped the mayor would proclaim as a holiday.[1]

This folk spirituality, severed from its theological and institutional roots, is at once a challenge and an opportunity for our congregations and their members. God does indeed love each of us, and angels do function as ministers of God's providence. These truths, however, are not more central to Christian convictions than other equally important truths. We are also fallible, limited, and given to an amazing variety of frivolities and the misjudgments of overheated and isolated imaginations. The isolation of angel experiences, their unconnectedness, continues to be troublesome. Some of these experiences seem overblown, elaborated, and verge on the bizarre; others seem trivialized and shallow. Some angel experiences fuel public skepticism, but at the same time present churches with issues of pastoral care they dare not ignore. Those men and women who have encountered an angel need also to encounter a loving and concerned community. When angels visit—individualism is not only not enough, it is dangerous. The task, then, is twofold: Angel experiences as spiritual events must be understood in such a way that they are integrated with other central expressions of the church's life, and the pastoral life of caring communities must include a ministry to the men and women whom angels visit.

To implement this ministry, pastors with their congregations must begin their task by thinking *theologically*, that is, considering how angels and angel experiences belong in the mission and purpose of the church's life in the world. The average Christian believer, surrounded as he or she is by the claims of a rampant individualism, needs to know how angels *connect*. Thinking *theologically* about angels means to understand where and how they fit into a larger biblical and doctrinal frame. Once that is understood and the theological ground is established with its own integrity, then insights on how to help, some borrowed from the social sciences, can be brought forward by pastors and other lay helpers to counsel those in need, one by one. If, on the other hand, the pastoral enterprise *begins* with something else, perhaps a premature borrowing from other disciplines, before and without theological integration, then American churches will have abandoned, once again, the wisdom and richness of their historical legacy.

I begin this discussion with an exposition of the angelology of Karl Barth and then bring forward the thought of an important contemporary, Carl Jung. I do so out of a general admiration for Barth's theological position on many fronts, but most especially because we have in him a powerful twentieth century Christian thinker who takes angels and angel encounters seriously, and then addresses who and what they are in God's grand scheme of things. He speaks to the dangers to be anticipated in viewing angels as "independent and autonomous subjects," disconnected from a congregational ministry and its theological and historical roots. Carl Jung, psychiatrist and religious thinker, populates the human psyche with an astonishing variety of characters: gurus, kings, queens, shamans, tricksters, warriors, among others, and angels which he, like Karl Barth, takes very seriously, having had a powerful personal experience with an angel-like creature he called Philemon. Jung, too, addresses the issue of independent angels on their own, and offers a warning as well as creative ideas the church might use in its own pastoral task.

Karl Barth (1886-1968), pastor and teacher in the Swiss Reformed Church, was described by Pope Pius XII as the greatest theologian since Thomas Aquinas. He is, certainly, the most influential theologian of the twentieth century. By Whitsunday in 1950, Barth had published the volume that included his angelology. In his *Church Dogmatics*, possibly the most impressive Protestant theological undertaking since the Reformation, Barth attempts a reconstruction of a denuded landscape. He picks up the issue of angels and restores them as a theme for serious theological study.

> It is true, of course, that we can...deny [angels] altogether. We can dismiss them as superfluous, or absurd and comic. We can protest with frowning brow and clenched fist that although we might admit that there is a God, it is going too far to allow that there are angels as well. They must be questioned or completely ignored.[2]

Barth is impressed with the weight and depth of the biblical witness.

> If we cannot or will not accept angels, how can we accept what is told us in Scripture, or the history of the Church, or the history of the Jews, or our own life's history? I will deal with this difficult subject because both Scripture and history demand it; but there are other important reasons as well: If angelology languishes, so too will our understanding of

God's Providence; and with the weakening of that doctrine, a serious distortion of the Christian faith will have occurred. Second, theological neglect of angelology contributes to a climate where angels may be viewed as having an autonomous existence of their own.[3]

Placing his angelology firmly under the doctrine of Providence in a final section, "The Kingdom of Heaven," Barth admits that the field of angelology is difficult. We may not even know how to ask the right questions, because angels exist at the very boundary of Christian knowledge; but it is vital that boundary be explored and something be said about the ministry of angels to humankind and to the world.

Barth begins his discussion with a brief history of how a doctrine of Providence entered the lexicon of Christian theology. It derives from Genesis 22:12-14, in which Abraham named the spot where an angel called to him and said,

> "Do not lay your hand on [Isaac] or do anything to him; for now I know that you fear God, since you have not withheld your son, your only son, from me."... Abraham went and took the ram and offered it up as a burnt offering instead of his son. So Abraham called that place "The Lord will provide."

The last words of the last sentence of the quotation, translated into Latin, are *Deus providebit*, or "God will provide," later glossed into "God's providence," and many hundreds of years later still, into a doctrine of "Providence."

God is faithful to his creation. Barth points out that God does not behave like a manufacturer who abandons what he makes after it is manufactured. Between God and the creation there is a bond that cannot be broken. He then quotes the lines of a German hymn as an exact statement of God's providential imperative:

That which the Lord our God did make,

> He surely will sustain;
> O'er all the way that it may take,
> His grace will always reign.[4]

Barth declares that every creature—every man, woman, and child on this planet—lives in the power of God's preservation and compassion. Barth does not mean that every human being is *reconciled* to God, but that God's active love for creation is directed against the threat of chaos and nothingness that hovers at the edge of reality. God, Barth assures us, will not allow creation to be overwhelmed by any hostile power, including the madness or the evil of human beings. The community of faith ought to find comfort in this providence. God will not allow us to destroy ourselves, but works in complex ways so that his goodness might be finally triumphant despite the wretched and disobedient abuse of human freedom.

Angels are God's ambassadors, and so long as they are understood that way, they fulfill their necessary function in God's covenant of preservation and grace.

> An ambassador...represents his government. He does not pursue any policy on his own, but only that of his government. He has no independent ideas or initiative. His activity consists wholly in representing as exactly and fully as possible the intentions of the government with which he has always to identify as his own. But while this is the sum of his activity, he represents his government with full authority. He is no mere emissary or official or commissar.[5]

Barth takes great pains to point out that although angels do not have the independence of citizens in the pursuit of their private concerns, they do represent the entire authority, majesty, and glory of God. He implies agreement with Thomas Aquinas that angels visit unbelievers as well as believers, the faithless as well as the faithful, and the lost and depraved as well as those who cling most faithfully to the promises of eternal life. In this instance, the difference between the Christian faithful and unbelievers is not that angels minister to one and not the other; it is that the faithful know in whose name the angel appears. Unbelievers may view this ministry as a sign of good luck or good fortune and give praise to no other than themselves. According to Barth, the Christian understands that the angel encounter is a triumph of the spirit.

> Listen to me, you stubborn of heart,
> you who are far from deliverance:
> I bring near my deliverance, it is not far off,
> and my salvation will not tarry (Isaiah 46:12-13).

The providence of God brings us to the notion of a personal guardian angel. Barth is uneasy with the idea, but he does not reject it out of hand. He asks why such a concept is necessary since God has already decreed his faithfulness and there are angels aplenty to do God's will and work. Individuals do not need a special private angel, he says, because all the hosts of heaven keep watch over us.

Barth suspects that guardian angels may be misused, especially when they are thought to give men and women spectacular help for their own plans by sending things that are pleasant and warding off those that are not. Angels are indeed present, but they make known God's help as to how each of us may participate personally and directly in God's covenant of grace.

Having prepared the ground for his angelology and planted it within a doctrine of Providence, Barth makes the point again and again that to ignore the issue of angels would be dangerous. He implies that those theologies that do ignore angels risk a religious catastrophe, because angels may come to be viewed as "independent and autonomous subjects." He does not speculate on the emerging cultural forms "independent and autonomous" angels might assume, but on the American scene, at least, the answer is clear. They have become a centerpiece for a folk spirituality, popularized in many guises, some unmercifully trivialized, others aggrandized in a variety of costumes and personalities.

The benevolent guardian angels of popular imagination—as portrayed in the motion picture series featuring Superman in his flowing cloak, and Batman with his bat wings (replacing the angel wings of an earlier day)—are engaged in a fierce fight with satanic violence, greed, and injustice. Superman is a timid, shy, even sexually innocent Mr. Everyman who is transformed into a creature of supernatural powers and pitted against terrestrial and extraterrestrial characters of villainous intent. Batman fights urban crime in Gotham City. Surrounded by a panoply of evil and seductive persons, he performs miraculous deeds of virtue in the name of the helpless and oppressed.

If anyone were to think that either Superman or Batman had lost any appeal, they might consider that Batman, a box-office hit, grossed more than $160,000,000 and Superman III brought Warner Brothers $142,000,000.

These larger-than-life characters, supernatural beings if you will, personifications by exaggeration of our human ideals of goodness, compassion, and justice, are dramatic and passionate models of these attributes, but they *are* exaggerations. No human being can be Superman or Batman and do what they do; yet, as righteous "angels" of goodness and mercy, they represent nothing beyond themselves in becoming an attractive distortion of our human nature.

Distortions that trivialize are as prevalent as those that inflate. A woman writes that she is well acquainted with her guardian angel, who is a constant companion. She says that while shopping for a special blouse for her married daughter she was directed to a particular store by "her" angel. When she arrived to make her purchase, she was told by the sales clerk that the blouse in the color and style she desired was sold out and no longer available. At that moment, she said, the angel whispered that such was not the case, that the blouse she wanted was, indeed, still available. The woman suggested that a further search be made, and, as the angel had predicted, the blouse she sought was found, having been mistakenly placed behind other blouses by another customer.

This story is as serious a distortion as Batman or Superman. In these cases the "angel" is severed not only from ecclesiastical concern, but from God as well. The woman's "angel" is helpful—as are Superman and Batman— but here the God of Abraham, Isaac, and Jacob has no transforming message to deliver. This "guardian angel," diminished and domesticated, reminds us of Barth's prophetic warning against angels as independent subjects severed from a God who is neither harmless nor familiar and who, while sustaining us, requires a reordering of every aspect of life.

A guardian angel, whether as Superhero or shopping companion, is a cultural efflorescence that could have been anticipated by another twentieth-century religious thinker: Carl Jung (1875-1961), psychiatrist and originator of analytical psychology, whose theories influence the spiritual and intellectual consciousness of millions of men and women in our own day. Carl Jung and Karl Barth were contemporaries, born within sixty-five miles of each other and steeped in the life of the Swiss Reformed Church. Jung had Swiss Reformed clergymen on both sides of his family. Two of his uncles were parsons, and there were no less than six on his mother's side. It is very likely that their families were acquainted with each other, although it is not known whether they ever met or spoke.

Each would see Superman or the shopping companion through very different lenses, but both might well claim a premonition of their appearance. Jung had the deeply held conviction that human beings yearn to connect with God and they will not rest until, in some fashion, they do. As a consequence, any number of mythological or spiritual figures might emerge from time to time as testimony to that unquenched thirst.

The appearance of these figures would also be an occasion for some worry, an expression of anxiety, and a warning. Both would be troubled by the autonomous, unconnected nature of their epiphany. Karl Barth might well have warned Christian believers again of the dreadful result to be expected from a continuation of the Protestant disdain for serious theological study of angels. Carl Jung might warn us that the appearance of "good" angels is a sign that the cultural emergence of mythical figures who are "bad" or "dark" angels is not far behind.

Jung discovered that as his patients neared the end of their treatment, their archetypal images included an awesome authority figure which he called the "god-imago." But the god-imago referred to an inner psychological experience and not necessarily to any objective reality. Jung himself never deviated from this position and, as did Karl Barth in regard to angels, refused to be drawn into controversy as to how God "exists."

> The idea of God is an absolutely necessary psychological function of an irrational nature and has nothing whatever to do with the question of God's existence. The human intellect can never answer this question, still less give any proof of God. Moreover, such proof is superfluous, for the idea of an all-powerful divine Being is present everywhere, unconsciously, if not consciously, because it is an archetype.[6]

Jung espouses a kind of psychological functionalism in that he is more interested in people's experiences of God than in any philosophical speculation on the existence or nonexistence of God, or of any other of the numerous mythological figures that excited his fascination. Once the god-imago or god archetype had been projected, experienced consciously, finally understood, and interpreted, then for Jung the process was completed.

Angels and demons reside in the depths of our unconscious, according to Jung, alongside the most ancient and universal "thought forms" or archetypes of humanity. The Angels, Archangels, Principalities, and Powers spoken of in Scripture and slumbering in our souls emerge from time to time in a form that *seems* to exist "out there" with a self-conscious existence. But they are, in fact, archetypal figures that emerge from our unconscious depths and form part of a hidden treasure upon which humankind has always drawn and from which it raised up its gods and demons and all the other religious thoughts without which we cease to be fully human.

Jung's perspective on our human situation is, in some respects, reminiscent of Martin Luther's. Human beings are participants in a battle between the forces of the "good angels" and the "dark angels." Satan, prince of the "dark angels," a most subtle creature, tries to influence Adam and Eve to be suspicious of God and to commit an act that frustrates God's purpose. Later, Satan in the form of a serpent or in myriad other cultural manifestations, continues his evil work. There is no end to Satan, as there is no end to "good angels" or to the Christ figure as a revelation of goodness and love.

Jung believed that when any religion, including Christianity, functions as it should, that religion embodies the projected inner God-image of the archetypal collective unconscious. The life forces of the inner self are mirrored in the external imagery the religion expresses in its mythology, liturgy and rites, and dogma. So long as the religion is able to contain these forces, its institutions, such as the church, protect its believers against the distortions to which fallible human beings are prone.

When a religion breaks down, when God is dead, religion loses its ability to carry the numerous individual projections invested in it. Then, men and women recall their projections back into themselves, and the stage is set for a crisis. Psychic energy previously invested now flows back into individual lives, and some very bad things can take place. There are numerous idolatrous possibilities available. There can be a reprojection into secular objects or political movements. Other more personal and noxious outcomes can include a most common distortion: an overdevelopment or inflation of one side of our personalities while another is submerged or ignored.

The antidote to these distortions induced by unconnected and autonomous archetypal images within the collective unconscious is a new synthesis into the whole. There needs to be a new integration, a rebalance of the inner archetypal forces. Some of Jung's modern adherents describe the possibilities of this new integration in arresting ways.

Robert Moore and Douglas Gillette, who discussed in detail the structures of the male psyche in their book, *The King Within*, then turn their attention to the feminine psyche:

> A woman's quadrated psyche functions just as does a man's. She balances the energies of four foundational archetypes—the Queen, Warrior, Magician, and Lover. The Queen guides a woman toward a centered calm, a sense of order she can extend into the outer world. She becomes gifted with the capacity to bless and join in fructifying union with other members of her "realm." The Warrior guides a woman in self-discipline and self-defense, and the defense of others.... The Magician affords a desire to introject, to raise and contain power, to heal and to act as mediator between the human and the divine spheres.... The Lover empowers a woman to be passionately and creatively engaged with all things, to be uninhibited sexually (playing and displaying) and profoundly spiritual.[8]

The archetypal symbols need each other for creative and harmonious balance, or in their autonomous mode they become warped and destructive. For example, when one of the male archetypes, the Warrior, is so caught, men tend to view certain female attitudes and behaviors as tyrannical and begin a struggle against them. Women are seen as necessary but inordinately powerful and normal male aggression may be contorted into a form of sadism until healing by integration and rebalance occurs.

All healing must be achieved by directing attention toward the energies and messages from the unconscious, including the collective unconscious, because these messages, appearing mostly in our dreams, have a purpose. They are the attempts of the unconscious to communicate something of great value, not only about the immediate and practical matters of one's personal or family life, but how we may be out of balance with the deepest life forces within us.

In his autobiography, *Memories, Dreams, Reflections,* Jung describes for us a very personal and powerful dream involving an angel-like figure he called Philemon.

> There was a blue sky, like the sea, covered not by clouds but by flat brown clods of earth. It looked as if the clods were breaking apart and the blue water of the sea were becoming visible between them. But the water was the blue sky. Suddenly there appeared from the right a winged being sailing across the sky. I saw that it was an old man with the horns of a bull. He held a bunch of four keys, one of which he clutched as if he were about to open a lock. He had the wings of a kingfisher with its character-istic colors.[9]

Jung said that at the time he did not understand the image of Philemon, and he painted it so he might study it further. Later, in a remarkable drawing, Jung depicted an old man with a long white beard and with shimmering blue wings overarching several trees of different varieties in a parklike setting. Above Philemon's head a halo appears, with a man-dala on each side. Jung tells us:

> Philemon and other figures of my fantasies brought home to me the crucial insight that there are things in the psyche which I do not produce, but which produce themselves and have their own life. Philemon represented a force which was not myself. In my fantasies I held conversations with him, and he said things which I had not consciously thought. For I observed clearly that it was he who spoke, not I. He said I treated thoughts as if I generated them myself, but in his view thoughts were like animals in the forest, or people in a room, or birds in the air, and

added, "If you should see people in a room, you would not think that you had made those people, or that you were responsible for them." It was he who taught me psychic objectivity, the reality of the psyche. Through him the distinction was clarified between myself and the object of my thought. He confronted me in an objective manner, and I understood that there is something in me which can say things that I do not know and do not intend, things which may even be directed against me.

Psychologically, Philemon represented superior insight. He was a mysterious figure to me. At times he seemed to me quite real, as if he were a living personality. I went walking up and down the garden with him, and to me he was what the Indians call a guru.[10]

Jung never ventured into a systematic angelology as did Karl Barth, but he easily could have. Philemon, a messenger from the *Imago Dei*, may remind Jung of an Indian guru, but to most of his European contemporaries Philemon behaves as would a guardian angel. A further elaboration on this messenger, or angel, theme might tempt an enterprising Jung theorist.

I have chosen, for the purposes of this book, to direct attention to Carl Jung as a *religious* thinker and as one of the two most creatively compelling for our time. Again and again, Jung comments and makes judgments on what he describes as the *Imago Dei* inside us and how the God-image addresses the destiny of every human being. Further, he and his contemporary, Karl Barth, understand that we receive destiny-changing messages from a center: the inner Imago Dei, to use Jung's term; or from God, "the wholly other," as used by Barth. These messages are of transcendent importance and are ignored or avoided at great peril.

Each of them believes that men and women are ineluctably religious, but more—that their religious landscape is populated. The images, characters, or subjects that populate the religious world defy attempts to make them into abstractions or axioms. The characters that populate the Bible or that inhabit the collective unconscious will not be extinguished. They appear in visions, dreams, and the strange secret encounters that often embarrass or alarm us.

Both Barth and Jung sense a grave danger in allowing any of the spiritual subjects they identify to languish on their own. Barth insists that an ignored angelology leads to catastrophe. The form and substance of the calamity is not only a truncated and misshaped theology, but what has already taken place: the attenuation of angels into cultural artifacts or men and women whose angel experiences stand isolated without the benefit of pastoral care from churches only dimly aware of the spiritual energies lost to them. Jung is equally prophetic. He declares that men and women in today's world have lost their souls in a cacophony of materialistic obsessions and need more religious intimacy with God who inhabits the deep center of their being. But our present condition is one of spiritual fragmentation in which the God image, projected outwards, appears in strange forms—some harmless, even helpful, as with Batman and Superman, and some also monstrous, diabolically monstrous, as found in a Hitler or a Stalin.

This discussion of two angelologies, developed in our own century by two powerful religious thinkers, brings us to an important juncture. I have viewed our present intellectual landscape, where men and women who have experienced an angel visitation find that experience isolated and "privatized," and I have drawn our attention to an earlier day when angels flourished and evoked a far different response. Angels ministered in full view and on center stage. That position has, since the Reformation, been replaced by a hesitant angelology and then by no angelology at all. Churches and congregations may have turned away from an interest in that subject; but, manifestly, many of their members have not. Seemingly undeterred, angels visit men and women today as they have for countless generations and give every indication they will continue that ministry. Karl Barth issues an important warning about angel encounters when that experience is unconnected to larger theological concerns and, as we have seen, reunites angels and angel encounters with the ancient doctrine of God's providence whereby angels are viewed as ministers and ambassadors of that providence. Carl Jung warns us of the personal inner perils to be expected from detached and unintegrated angels, and he describes how fragmented parts of our souls, including angel archetypes, require a more connected and harmonious whole.

These two religious understandings, in many ways philosophically at odds with each other, provide important agreements and warnings and a frame: an inner and an outer, a theological and a psychological perspective for the issues that will occupy the rest of this book. How might those who have angel experiences, like Jane and Philip, be brought into the spiritual and liturgical life of real American congregations? And how might these men and women contribute to the vitality of local congregations while opening themselves to the wisdom and discipline of the church's legacy of knowledge and experience designed for the nurture and care of those whom angels visit?

## Notes

1. *Washington Post,* "Under Wing: Angel Followers Set Aside Day to Celebrate Spiritual Guardians," 21 Aug. 1993.

2. Karl Barth, *Church Dogmatics,* vol. III, part 3, trans. G. W. Bromiley and R.J. Ehrlich (Edinburgh: T. & T. Clark, 1960), 238.

3. Idem.

4. Ibid., 13.

5. Ibid., 512-513.

6. Carl G. Jung, "Two Essays on Analytical Psychology," from *Collected Works: Carl G. Jung,* The Bollingen Series, vol. VII, ed. by Herbert Read, Michael Fordham, Gerhard Adler (New York: Pantheon Books, 1953), 70.

7. Edward F. Edinger, *Ego and Archetype* (Boston: Shambhala Press, 1992), 6.

8. Robert Moore and Douglas Gillette, *The King Within* (New York: William Morrow & Co., 1992), 279.

9. Carl G. Jung, *Memories, Dreams, Reflections* (New York: Vintage Books, 1989), 182-183.

10. Ibid., 183.

# CHAPTER V

# The Biblical Witness

Angels function as ministers of God's providence. But the church community needs to know more if it is to contribute pastorally in the lives of men and women who live with the pressures and opportunities of real life. The church and its pastors need to know *how* angels behave as ministers of that Providence. Is there an identifiable style, a characteristic mode of angelic expression one can know and trust? The question is a crucial one for the church and for believers. Angel encounters can, as we have seen, descend into trivia and inflate into monstrosities, and they are prone to every inventive distortion our fallible human minds are capable of producing. How, then, can congregations and their pastors begin their pastoral ministry to those with angelic encounters unless they have some measurement, some categories of assessment to discern good spirits from distorted ones and genuine angel experiences from the mistaken notions of an overexcited imagination?

There is a way. We can turn, first, to Scripture, as the church's thinkers and theologians have done since its earliest days. Angels are everywhere in the Bible, for the authors of all the canonical books view angels as an inextricable part of their story. Angels are faithful messengers and agents who carry out God's will. The Hebrew word *Malakh* and the Greek *angelos*, common terms that appear in both linguistic cultures, mean "messenger." In the book of Genesis alone there are nine references to angels, and in the Old Testament as a whole, forty-seven encounters with angels are recorded by biblical authors.

Angels are inseparable from New Testament narrations as well. An angel announces the birth of Jesus. Angels minister to Christ before his temptation and in his agony at Gethsemane. They declare his resurrection and his ascension. There are more than seventy such angelic appearances narrated by New Testament authors.

The Bible does not present us with a fully developed angelology, but angels play a pivotal role in the dozens of narrative actions where they are featured. An examination of these narratives reveals six operational or stylistic characteristics common to all of them. These distinctive traits are a critical ingredient not only for the development of a pastoral theology of angel encounters but as a means to approach a judgment on the authenticity of those encounters even in our own day.

First: Angels pronounce warnings and deliver admonishments, but their most decisive messages are good news. Angels are the bearers of *glad tidings*—the original "evangelists."

Hagar, Sarah's slave girl, runs away from home because she is pregnant with Abraham's child and fearful of Sarah's vengeance. An angel finds her in the wilderness, tells her to return home, and announces:

> "I will so greatly multiply your offspring that they
> cannot be counted for the multitude....
> Now you have conceived and shall bear a son;
>    you shall call him Ishmael,
>    for the Lord has given heed to your affliction.
> He shall be a wild ass of a man,
> with his hand against everyone,
>    and everyone's hand against him;
> and he shall live at odds with all his kin"
> (Genesis 16:10-12).

Later in Genesis the author produces one of the most dramatic of all the angel narratives: God's command that Abraham sacrifice his son, Isaac.

> When they came to the place that God had

shown him, Abraham built an altar there and laid the wood in order. He bound his son Isaac, and laid him on the altar, on top of the wood. Then Abraham reached out his hand and took the knife to kill his son. But the angel of the Lord called to him from heaven, and said, "Abraham, Abraham!" And he said, "Here I am." [The angel] said, "Do not lay your hand on the boy or do anything to him; for now I know that you fear God, since you have not withheld your son, your only son, from me... because you have done this.... I will indeed bless you, and I will make your offspring as numerous as the stars of heaven and as the sand that is on the seashore "

(Genesis 22:9-17).

God sends his angel Gabriel to Nazareth to address a young woman named Mary and to deliver astounding news. Nazareth is a town on the north border of the Plain of Esdraelon, of no great importance and possibly of bad reputation. Mary is engaged to a pious and kindly man, Joseph, a carpenter. She is a virgin, a simple woman, and the New Testament gives us little information about her. Yet in this improbable place and to this unpretentious person, Gabriel announces a miracle of transcendent importance.

The angel begins with a salutation: "Greetings, favored one! The Lord is with you." Mary does not expect an angel and is startled. Gabriel continues:

"Do not be afraid, Mary, for you have found favor with God. And now, you will conceive in your womb and bear a son, and you will name him Jesus. He will be great, and will be called the Son of the Most High, and the Lord God will give to him the throne of his ancestor David. He will reign over the house of Jacob forever, and of his kingdom there will be no end."

> Mary said to the angel, "How can this be,
> since I am a virgin?" The angel said to her,
> "The Holy Spirit will come upon you, and
> the power of the Most High will overshadow
> you; therefore the child to be born will be
> holy; he will be called Son of God"
> (Luke 1:30-35).

After this glorious announcement, while visiting with her cousin Elizabeth, Mary breaks into rapturous song:

> "My soul magnifies the Lord,
>     and my spirit rejoices in God my Savior,
> for he has looked with favor on the lowliness
>     of his servant.
> Surely, from now on, all generations will call
>     me blessed" (Luke 1:47-48).

Angels bear news that induces jubilation, even ecstasy, for the blessings they announce are beyond our human abilities to bring them to pass: One's progeny will become a multitude; an only son is spared; a woman who has never known a man will give birth to a child to be called "Son of the Most High." Yet the vocabularies of jubilation have a second expression—worship, with angels in adoration leading the blessed in praise and thanksgiving.

Second: Angels are faithful witnesses to God and lead men and women toward increasing devotion and worship. In most Old Testament narratives angels appear in human form, always male and without wings. They speak, they eat, and they fight. But the book of Ezekiel is illustrative of another tradition. Angels are described as having wings and being grouped in adoration around the heavenly throne as worshipers and guardians of sacred things. These angels are called Cherubim by some biblical authors, and in Isaiah they are called Seraphim.

The writer of Ezekiel dates Ezekiel's vision in a very precise manner. It occurred in the thirteenth year, on the fifth day of the fourth month, among the exiles in Babylon along the river Chebar. Ezekiel says he saw a great cloud with brightness around it and:

> fire flashing forth continually, and in the middle of the fire...four living creatures...they were of human form. Each had four faces, and each of them, had four wings.... Under their wings on their four sides they had human hands.... As for the appearance of their faces: the four had the face of a human being, the face of a lion on the right side, the face of an ox on the left side, and the face of an eagle; such were their faces (Ezekiel 1:4-8, 10-11).

These mysterious, angel-like creatures, tireless and faithful attendants, surround the throne of God and worship, while the exile, far from home, rejoices in that vision.

The book of Revelation takes up a similar theme except that now it is Jesus, the Lamb of God, who is surrounded by angels leading in worship and praise a massive chorus that includes animals, fish, and any other undesignated creatures that may live under the earth.

> Then I looked, and I heard the voice of many angels surrounding the throne and the living creatures and the elders; they numbered myriads of myriads and thousands of thousands, singing with a full voice,
> " Worthy is the Lamb that was slaughtered, to receive power and wealth and wisdom and might and honor and glory and blessing!"
> Then I heard every creature in heaven and on earth and under the earth and in the sea, and all that is in them, singing,
> " To the one seated on the throne and to the Lamb be blessing and honor and glory and might forever and ever!"
> And the four living creatures said, "Amen!"

And the elders fell down and worshiped
(Revelation 5:11-14).

These fantastic creatures had a long and rich evolution in
later liturgical tradition. This portion of the Catholic Mass,
and subsequent modifications in other traditions, begins with
the *Sursum Corda*, raising the congregation into the realms of
angelic hosts praising God:

The bishop or priest faces the congregation and says:

| Celebrant: | Lift up your hearts. |
|---|---|
| People: | We lift them up unto the Lord. |
| Celebrant: | Let us give thanks unto our Lord God. |
| People: | It is meet and right so to do. |

Facing the altar, the celebrant proceeds:

> It is very meet, right, and our bounden duty,
> that we should at all times, and in all places,
> give thanks to thee, O Lord, holy Father,
> almighty, everlasting God.
>
> Therefore with Angels and Archangels, and
> with all the company of heaven, we laud and
> magnify thy glorious Name; evermore prais-
> ing thee, and saying,
>
> Holy, holy, holy, Lord God of Hosts:
> Heaven and earth are full of thy glory,
> Glory be to thee, O Lord Most High.

The liturgical scholar Dom Gregory Dix speculated that
the *Sanctus* (Holy, holy, holy), taken from Isaiah's vision in
the sixth century before Christ, had already found its way into
Christian liturgy by the third century as an angelic hymn and
was there preserved in the Catholic Mass and later in *The
Book of Common Prayer*.

The *Sanctus* is familiar, perhaps overfamiliar, to those of us who worship in liturgically centered congregations. We sing "Holy, holy, holy," but we tend to lose intensity, not only because we sing it regularly week by week, but because we cannot really conceive of singing *with* the angels and archangels as did third century believers who thought of themselves as *joined* with the angels in heaven while they sang. This rhapsodic vocabulary of angelic discourse, embedded as it has been for more than sixteen hundred years in a liturgy, does give us a glimpse of how an ancient people entered into their own experience with the angelic hosts.

Third: An angel encounter is a life-transforming event. Viewed in biblical perspective, angels do not give themselves to a Get-to-Know-Your-Guardian-Angel Day. An angel experience is never peripheral or lacking in substance or intensity. Consider the very old and dramatic tale found in the book of Genesis. Jacob is returning to his native soil after having escaped from his brother, Esau, whom he had tricked out of his birthright and paternal blessing. Jacob is terrified to learn that Esau, accompanied by four hundred men, is planning to meet him; anticipating Esau's rage, Jacob sends out his emissaries with many gifts to pacify his brother.

> The same night [Jacob] got up and took his two wives, his two maids, and his eleven children, and crossed the ford of the Jabbok. He took them and sent them across the stream, and likewise everything that he had. Jacob was left alone; and a man wrestled with him until daybreak. When the man saw that he did not prevail against Jacob, he struck him on the hip socket; and Jacob's hip was put out of joint as he wrestled with him. Then he said, "Let me go, for the day is breaking." But Jacob said, "I will not let you go, unless you bless me." So he said to him, "What is your name?" And he said, "Jacob." Then the man said, "You shall no longer be called Jacob, but Israel" (Genesis 32:22ff).[1]

Jacob leaves this harrowing scene to meet his brother, limping with his broken hip and with a guilty conscience. There is a reconciliation. "Esau ran to meet him, and embraced him, and fell on his neck and kissed him, and they wept" (33:4).

This is not the first story involving an angel recorded in the book of Genesis, but it is, surely, one of the most dramatic. The story is an episode in a larger story—Jacob's swindle of Esau's birthright—but we are drawn to notice the primitive strangeness of this portion of the narrative. The angel does not appear benign. He is male, athletic, and certainly dangerous. Jacob and the angel engage in an all-night wrestling match. In the struggle, the angel wounds Jacob, who bears his mutilation with astonishing equanimity and then demands that he be blessed. The angel does so by announcing that Jacob's name will be changed. He is to be called *Israel*, meaning "the one who strives with God."

Wrestling with the angel on the bank of the Jabbok is a turning point in the Jacob-Israel saga, and the mutilation is a sign that nothing will ever be the same. Jacob is marked forever, and there remains only one issue: How will Israel, his progeny, and his kin respond to the new identity? Jacob, now Israel, locked in struggle with God, will be the material the authors of Genesis will carefully document for many of that book's fifty chapters.

Instances of the destiny-transforming consequences of angel visits abound in both the Old and New Testaments: Names are changed, personalities are established, progeny is promised. The angel appearance is fraught with intensity and meaning. The angel, the good ambassador of God, announces new directions and new life after which nothing, absolutely nothing, will ever be as it was.

Fourth: As champions of God's people, angels protect human beings and help them fulfill their destiny as brave and faithful believers. Elijah's life was in danger. He had been threatened by the powerful Jezebel, who vowed to have him killed. He fled into the wilderness and, alone and in despair, asked God to let him die. Suddenly, an angel appeared and said:

"Get up and eat." [Elijah] looked, and there at his head was a cake baked on hot stones, and a jar of water. He ate and drank, and lay down again. The angel of the Lord came a second time, touched him, and said, "Get up and eat, otherwise the journey will be too much for you." He got up, and ate and drank; then he went in the strength of that food forty days and forty nights to Horeb the mount of God (1 Kings 19:5-8).

Daniel has been betrayed by jealous rivals in the court of Darius, king of the Persians. Daniel has broken a law having to do with religious observances and must be punished. He is sealed in a cave with hungry lions while Darius says, "May your God, whom you faithfully serve, deliver you!" (Daniel 6:16). Daniel survives the ordeal, declaring, "my God sent his angel and shut the lions' mouths so that they would not hurt me, because I was found blameless before him; and also before you, O king. I have done no wrong" (6:19-22).

Alone on the Mount of Olives, Jesus is about to enter the trials of his betrayal and crucifixion. He is in great distress and prays, "Father, if you are willing, remove this cup from me; yet, not my will but yours be done." An angel appears, ministers to him, and gives him strength (Luke 22:42-43f).

Food miraculously appears, lions are tamed, a moment of extraordinary anguish is broken into by a helping hand; so, Scripture gives testimony to the caring and protection of God's angels. But these good angels are not the only angels who interact with their human counterparts in this fallen world. There is another angel-like being, neither faithful nor friendly: Satan, who will be called the devil or Lucifer and who functions as the ruler of an earthly counterculture of evil.

The development of Satan as the evil one did not happen all at once. In the Old Testament, Satan was not the Satan we now know. In the book of Job, Satan is the accuser in God's heavenly courthouse.

One day the heavenly beings came to present

themselves before the Lord, and Satan also
came among them. The Lord said to Satan,
"Where have you come from?" Satan
answered the Lord, "From going to and fro
on the earth, and from walking up and down
on it." The Lord said to Satan, "Have you
considered my servant Job? There is no one
like him on the earth, a blameless and upright
man who fears God and turns away from
evil." Then Satan answered the Lord, "Does
Job fear God for nothing? Have you not put a
fence around him and his house and all that he
has, on every side? You have blessed the work
of his hands, and his possessions have
increased in the land. But stretch out your
hand now, and touch all that he has, and he
will curse you to your face." The Lord said to
Satan, "Very well, all that he has is in your
power; only do not stretch out your hand
against him." So Satan went out from the
presence of the Lord (Job 1:6-12).

It is not until the intertestamental period that Satan took
on his evil role. Broadly speaking, the New Testament did not
add much to Old Testament understanding of angels, but the
authors who wrote these books seem to have been aware of a
new idea: Satan was, indeed, the evil one, and they hinted at
the thought that he had been an angel who was expelled from
heaven because of his disobedience. The author of Luke has
the seventy appointed by Jesus say:

"Lord, in your name even the demons submit
to us!" [Jesus] said to them, "I watched Satan
fall from heaven like a flash of lightning. See,
I have given you all authority...over the power
of the enemy; and nothing will hurt you"
(Luke 10:17-19).

The idea of Satan as a fallen angel produced a florid, theological speculation in the writings of those who followed New Testament authors and, later, in Martin Luther, as we have seen. Luther viewed Satan, an evil and clever spiritual being, as humankind's most dangerous enemy, and every living person—man, woman, and child—was exhorted to seek the guidance and protection of God's good angels who would minister to them from birth and through their death.

Fifth: Angels bring to light the meanings of mysterious or hidden events. They can interpret dreams. The author of the thirty-first chapter of Genesis tells us that the sons of Laban are becoming jealous so that Jacob and his family are threatened. Jacob says:

> "During the mating of the flock I once had a dream in which I looked up and saw that the male goats that leaped upon the flock were striped, speckled, and mottled. Then the angel of God said to me in the dream, 'Jacob,' and I said, 'Here I am!' And [the angel] said, 'Look up and see that all the goats that leap on the flock are striped, speckled, and mottled; for I have seen all that Laban is doing to you. I am the God of Bethel, where you anointed a pillar and made a vow to me. Now leave this land at once and return to the land of your birth'" (Genesis 31:10-13).

The book of Matthew tells us an angel spoke directly to Joseph in a dream and warned him to flee from King Herod and escape into Egypt.

> An angel of the Lord appeared to Joseph in a dream and said, "Get up, take the child and his mother, and flee to Egypt, and remain there until I tell you; for Herod is about to search for the child, to destroy him." Then Joseph got up, and took the child and his mother by night, and went to Egypt, and remained there until the death of Herod (Matthew 2:13-15).

Mary Magdalene and another woman go to the tomb where Jesus is interred. The ground trembles, and an angel appears who rolls away the stone blocking the entrance. The appearance of the angel is terrifying to all those present, including the soldiers who guard the tomb. The angel says:

> "Do not be afraid; I know that you are look-
> ing for Jesus who was crucified. He is not
> here; for he has been raised, as he said. Come,
> see the place where he lay. Then go quickly
> and tell his disciples, 'He has been raised from
> the dead, and indeed he is going ahead of you
> to Galilee; there you will see him'"
> (Matthew 28:5-7).

These stories express moments of surpassing intensity. Something new has happened. The structures of life have been broken into and new directions are revealed. Jacob is to return to his homeland; Joseph is to leave his; the body of a crucified Jesus is no longer where it ought to be.

Sixth: Angels are never anticipated, and both their appearance and messages are surprising. The human subjects are almost always incredulous. The angel is reassuring, "Don't be afraid," he says to Mary, who has just learned that her pregnancy, which she did not believe possible, was about to happen and was to have consequences of such magnitude as to defy imagination. The tomb of a dead man is now empty and the dead man resurrected. This is stunning, possibly precarious, so reassurance is necessary: "Fear not!"

The encounter itself cannot be forecast nor the angel's message foretold. In ordinary life we human beings think things through, either with ourselves or with others and then we decide on some hoped for outcome. Real life is the story of its vicissitudes and we are often surprised by an unanticipated result but angel encounters are by their nature surprising and the Bible takes pains to underscore that characteristic. All angel encounters are confrontational. Angelic speech tends then to be direct, declarative and revelatory: "You will conceive," "Your name is Israel," "Eat and drink," and so forth.

Neither Mary, nor Hagar, nor Jacob, nor Daniel control the encounter or have the upper hand. They participate in the angelic action but they do not determine its direction or manage it in any way.

The angel appears, a pronouncement is forthcoming, but it is in response to the confrontation that the narrative action continues. The angel never asks Mary how she feels or thinks about being pregnant, or Jacob about whether or not he objects to his new name but how they do respond to the angel, God's ambassador, is a serious matter indeed. Various authors have been so transfixed by the high drama and consummate meaning of how they and others responded that they produced an entire library of books, comprising our Bible, to tell the story.

Scripture views these six characteristics of angelic encounter as normative. However, there are other biblical perspectives that illuminate broader theological issues in regard to our human condition and the angels who encounter us. Biblical authors view the men and women whom angels visit in a very different way than we do today. There is no *self*-possessed individual in biblical literature. Human life does not own itself. It belongs to God, as do all other forms of life. The authors of our Bible find it unimaginable that a self belonging to itself might exist. There is no private "I" in Scripture. There are solitary hunters or travelers but they live temporarily dangerous lives. To be solitary is to be in fearful peril. It can mean detachment, exile and death.

We belong to God and not to ourselves, but this does not diminish human life or the value of each person, nor does it require a loss of personal self-esteem. In an extraordinary story found in Genesis 18 and 19, God confides in Abraham concerning the destruction of Sodom. Then one of the most astounding conversations in all of literature takes place. Abraham engages God in a dialogue designed to change God's mind about what he is about to do. Knowing that he is but dust and ashes as compared with Yahweh, Abraham draws near and says:

"Will you indeed sweep away the righteous with

the wicked? Suppose there are fifty righteous within the city; will you then sweep away the place and not forgive it for the fifty righteous who are in it? Far be it from you to do such a thing, to slay the righteous with the wicked, so that the righteous fare as the wicked! Far be that from you! Shall not the Judge of all the earth do what is just?" And the Lord said, "If I find at Sodom fifty righteous in the city, I will forgive the whole place for their sake." Abraham answered, "Let me take it upon myself to speak to the Lord, I who am but dust and ashes. Suppose five of the fifty righteous are lacking? Will you destroy the whole city for lack of five?" And he said, "I will not destroy it if I find forty-five there." Again he spoke to him, "Suppose forty are found there." He answered, "For the sake of forty I will not do it." Then he said, "Oh do not let the Lord be angry if I speak. Suppose thirty are found there." He answered, "I will not do it, if I find thirty there." He said, "Let me take it upon myself to speak to the Lord. Suppose twenty are found there." He answered, "For the sake of twenty I will not destroy it." Then he said, "Oh do not let the Lord be angry if I speak just once more. Suppose ten are found there." He answered, "For the sake of ten I will not destroy it" (Genesis 18:23-32).

Apparently, the narrator concluded, this is a final limit. God will not go from ten innocent to five innocent and finally to one. "And the Lord went his way, when he had finished speaking to Abraham; and Abraham returned to his place"(18:33).

Gerhard von Rad, a celebrated Old Testament scholar, observes that the passage is heavily burdened with a problem of credibility:[2] "Will you indeed sweep away the righteous with the wicked...Shall not the Judge of all the earth do what is just?" That a human being, constituted of dust and ashes, should be so bold as to attempt to change God's understanding of his own intentions *is* unbelievable. Yet, such is God's respect for Abraham that he is allowed to do so.

Modernity's mistake is to have imagined God as an alien being—"out there"—like a ghostly object far away in space whom to serve is to lose our personhood and our freedom. It is a profundity of our Hebrew-Christian understanding of human life that although we belong to God and live and die in his providence, we are yet free. Indeed, it is a conviction of that faith to declare that insofar as we are faithful sojourners in God's providence we are most liberated, most free, and most ourselves.

In this chapter we have examined how Scripture views angel appearances: *Angels are God's messengers*; they lead toward a *strengthening of one's faith;* an angel encounter produces *life-transforming changes*; angels are *life-protecting* and supportive; angels *disclose* vitally important information about one's destiny in life that has been obscured or hidden; an angel encounter cannot be programmed—it is always *unanticipated.* How, then, can these characteristics become benchmarks for a congregation-based pastoral ministry, and how can those men and women who experience an angel encounter profit from such care? It is these large and central issues that will occupy the rest of this book.

## Notes

1. This very old account reports that a "man" wrestled with Jacob. Later interpretation tended to view this "man" as an angel; so, we find in Hosea 12:2-4:
   The Lord has an indictment against Judah,
      and will punish Jacob according to his ways,
      and repay him according to his deeds.
   In the womb he tried to supplant his brother,
      and in his manhood he strove with God.
   He strove with the angel and prevailed.
2. See: Gerhard von Rad, *Genesis* (London: SCM Press, 1972), 213ff.

# CHAPTER VI

# Beginnings

Socially sensitive churches and synagogues sometimes drift into a single-minded spirit of community service, of providing good things such as day care centers, professional counseling services, programs for the poor and homeless, and, in particularly lively congregations, many more expressions of their compassionate ministry. There is nothing wrong with this outreach or with congregations who make it possible. Most frequently missed, however, are the marvelous spiritual energies that congregations and their pastors have available within their midst. Men and women inhabit these congregations who, unseen and unnoticed, could testify to powerful spiritual experiences of redemption and healing. This is not a small thing. The church, a colony of believers who witness to the saving power of God in human life, has within its membership those who have first-hand personal experience with this power, yet who remain isolated and alone and whose extraordinary encounter with an angel sent by God is unknown and unappreciated.

It will not be easy for the church to reach out by reaching *within* to begin this reconciliation. There is much to overcome: decades of neglect; an unrelenting intellectual skepticism about angel experiences, both within congregations and in the general population; a lack of useful models for a pastoral ministry to men and women whom angels visit; and, not least, the mistrust of churchly intentions by those who most need congregational and pastoral support.

How to begin? I offer several examples of a *pastoral*

approach to men and women who claim an angel encounter. All of them, except one, are taken from my own caseload, including the experience of a Methodist clergyman whom I first counseled during his seminary education. One is a model of the valuable service the church and its pastoral ministry might offer a confused soul who claims to have heard an angel's voice. Another is an example of pastoral work with a couple, in which a husband hid behind his angel experience and damaged his marriage. None of these pastoral endeavors involves the worship or educational life of any congregation, but each is a beginning, demonstrating pastoral counseling in action and the spiritual energies available to a more alert and commodious church.

Talmage Bandy is a student chaplain in a training hospital located in Alexandria, Virginia. This account in a letter to me could, she said, have had a title, "Walking Dark Corridors to Light."

> Walking the corridors of a city hospital as a chaplain is not unlike walking a tightrope of faith. You wonder if the net is under you. From one second to the next, anything can happen—a healthy baby can be born, a sick baby can die while an old lady clings tenaciously to life, a fire can break out, a Code Blue can be sounded. The nights can be still or they can be fraught with disaster. You can be called when you least expect it or want it. Life ebbs and flows. You find yourself wondering where God's holy angels are hiding, and you pray that God walks beside you, but you're not sure. You remember your teacher saying that God is in the hospital room when you enter, and He is there when you leave, and you are humbled.

> Something happened to me last week. I was conscious of when it happened; I'm just not

sure *how* it happened. Later I laughed because although I avoid religious talk, I was wearing my red shoes, what my friend calls my "Holy Spirit shoes." The hour was late, time for me to return to the chaplain's office, make my log entry, and leave the hospital. It had been noted several days earlier that a certain patient, an Episcopalian, had said that she missed receiving the Holy Communion. It had also been recorded that she had been too tired for a visit from the chaplain that day. There were other patients to see, plenty to keep me busy, and yet, I decided to stop in to see her.

Upon entering her room I found a crone-like, querulous old woman, her face withered and ugly with years of being miserable and malcontented. She immediately ordered me to sit down and began a litany of complaints directed first at the staff and then at every job and every person she had ever known. She was a thoroughly unlovable and unlikeable person. My thoughts were racing: "Why had I bothered to see this patient?" When I left her room to get her some ice I asked a particular nurse whom I call Saint Joan if she was Ms. C's nurse, aware that we are not allowed to give a patient anything without permission from the medical staff. "Thank God," she responded, "not tonight." My sympathy was with the nurse. When I asked the patient if she would like the Holy Communion, she declined, and each time I attempted to leave she begged me to stay, demanded that I stay, and continued to complain. My eyes were on the wall clock; I wanted to leave in the worst kind of way and check on my favorite unit, the Intensive Care Nursery. It was then that it happened. A calmness came over me and I felt my body relax. I turned myself totally over to her and looked long and hard into her distorted face. Could this be me someday—wild-haired, grotesque, gnarled, miserable? My life has been too happy and too good for me to turn as bitter and sour as she, but I began to see her as a human being loved by God if not by me. When I finally prepared to leave her, I said that I was sorry she had not let me bring the Eucharist to her. It then became apparent that she had declined because she feared I would leave and not return. When I explained that I didn't have to leave the hospital, only go to the chaplain's office, then, ah! she wanted it. It even occurred to me that she really didn't care about the Eucharist, that it was a way of keeping me there a bit longer. When I returned to her room with the small communion set, she had managed to pull herself to a partial sitting position with her legs dangling off the side of the bed. Although more slumping than sitting, I sensed an effort on her part to add dignity and reverence to the occasion. I cleaned off her table full of cups and dirty tissues, washed my hands, and set up a small altar. As I removed the small chalice from the box, I explained what I was doing, although her head hung so low that we could not see each other's faces. She became quiet as I began the words of the Prayer Book, and she attempted to repeat some of the familiar prayers after me, including the Lord's Prayer. The brittleness left her voice.

When we had finished she eased herself back to a lying position saying: "I'm glad we did that. My angel who watches over me sent you to see me tonight." She even expressed concern over me driving home so late at night and cautioned me to be careful. Concern for me. I am convinced that she was transformed, if only for a moment, by some power from God. I am not always aware of the presence of God, but I believe it was there in full force that night. Was it possible that, improbable as it seems, I was, for one brief instant, sent by that angel as an instrument of His peace?

Talmage Bandy's remarkable pastoral visit, honest and beautifully written, is exceptional, but it is not rare. The testimony of a personal experience involving an angel is to be found in many places both within and outside American churches and synagogues. Parish clergy might themselves find numerous examples of parishioners who can recount transforming experiences of an angelic encounter. They are everywhere. I have information from men and women who give witness of angelic healing: a wife whose husband has lymphatic leukemia; a woman with a perforated gallbladder; a man who had open-heart surgery. There are testimonials about angels who inspired hope where hopelessness and despair had destroyed the energy and will to live. There are letters by men and women who unexpectedly found peace and fulfillment where none had existed. One woman described how an angel assisted her in finding a "wonderful man," who proposed marriage when she had given up the search. Some were ministered to by an angel in such a way as to rediscover feelings of love and devotion toward a spouse or a child or a parent when such feelings had been dissolved into bitterness or recrimination. Angels do, indeed, minister to people with a remarkably wide range of the woes and tribulations that afflict the human spirit.

However, I return to Talmage Bandy's account to illustrate a central issue of this investigation of angels and angel encounters. There is a Christian and biblical perspective on such encounters, and it is this perspective I develop, using the pastoral visit Talmage Bandy wrote about.

First: The patient herself identifies the one who guards her and addresses her. "My angel who watches over me sent you to see me tonight," she says. This is not by itself sufficient, nor is any other criterion alone sufficient to confirm an angel experience as authentic, but it is a promising beginning. It is possible, I suppose, to have a spiritual encounter and not identify it as the angelic visit it really is. The author of the book of Hebrews reminds us to show hospitality to strangers, because by doing so we may entertain angels without knowing it (Hebrews. 13:2). However, a long and well-documented pastoral tradition *does* inform us that satanic or fallen angels encounter human beings disguised as good angels as they seek to subvert our hearts and our lives. Could this be the situation here? It is imaginatively possible, but the case for this being a good and faithful angel continues to build.

Second: The angel appears to have no independent agenda of its own and is clearly understood as a minister of God's love. The old woman says that the angel sent the chaplain to visit her, and the chaplain is, obviously, a representative of the church's pastoral and sacramental ministry. The chaplain celebrates the Lord's Supper, they pray the Lord's Prayer, and the patient confesses, "I'm glad we did that." The chaplain is herself convinced that something healthy and good has taken place and remarks that as improbable as it seems, it is possible that an angel sent her to this "malcontented" and "unlovable" person as an instrument of God's peace.

Third: As a corollary to the angel's providential action, something is required of the patient. She is called upon to respond, to do something or be something—to change. The old woman cannot remain as she was before the angel acted. Guardian angels as *God's* ambassadors want an answer that is appropriate to the message, namely, to be a more faithful and obedient disciple of the Providence that dispatched the ambassador. In this event, the old woman does respond; she relaxes, "the brittleness [leaves] her voice," she eases herself back into a lying position, and she expresses concern for the chaplain's welfare, a startling change of attitude and behavior.

Fourth: The episode catches both the patient and the chaplain off balance. They had not anticipated the encounter or the consequences. The old woman had not expected the chaplain to care enough to stay with her. The chaplain is surprised to realize that this difficult person is ready to receive the Eucharist, and then later surprised when the patient warns her about driving home late at night. Grace seems to have come to them in a way that neither the patient nor the chaplain has anticipated.

They were both surprised, but the timing was exquisitely right. That is, they were prepared for that particular kind of surprise. Angels are always on time, every time. Their actions occur at the exact moment when their subjects are ready to change. Angels heed the wise biblical injunction not to cast pearls before swine. The chaplain and her patient are at that mysterious moment when life is ready to erupt into new configurations and meanings—a new form of life or a new way of being, something that is, perhaps, improbable. The chaplain is visiting a patient who has the reputation of being an "unlikeable person" and finds herself wanting to skip the visit altogether. The patient begins by whining, complaining, and refusing the offered Eucharist. The arriving, grace-filled moment begins in the most unpromising way, but, improbable as it might be, it does arrive.

This letter from Mark, a Methodist minister and client I had seen for counseling three years earlier, came as a welcome surprise:

> I just had to write when I heard from Dr. _____ that you were doing some research on angels, and if you can handle one more angel story I want to tell you about mine. Louise and I are still together but not much differently than before. As you very well know, our relationship has been discouraging for a long time. After we left therapy with you, Louise and I talked about divorce—I even went to see a lawyer, but I somehow knew inside my heart that I did not have the courage to go through with it. I was desperate. Our farce of a marriage dragged on and on right in the face of the whole congrega-

tion. I felt like a failure and a hypocrite, and I prayed to God, but nothing happened. I beseeched God day after day to please help me—anything that would save my marriage.

Then one night at around 2 A.M. I had a wonderful spiritual experience. I went to bed emotionally exhausted. Louise and I had ended our day with another of our terrible disagreements. I thought she had been too flirty with a neighbor. I said so, and of course she denied it—sounds familiar to you, I'm sure. It was awful. Anyhow, I woke up and the whole bedroom was filled with a golden light. It was not moonlight—and there at the foot of my bed was a figure, an angel sent by God—I'm sure of that. The angel looked at me intensely with wide-open eyes maybe for fifteen seconds. I had goose bumps all over my body, and I wanted to cry. I couldn't take my eyes off this angel, and I heard words in my mind that said, "I am with you always." Then the angel disappeared. The whole experience was miraculous, and I was so excited I got up without waking Louise and went down on my knees to thank God for touching my life in such a marvelous way.

After reading Mark's long letter (longer than this excerpted portion), I telephoned, thanked him for keeping in touch, and invited him to visit me for further discussion of his angel experience. Mark's congregation is a long 180 miles from my home near Washington, D.C., but he did come and continued with counseling for five sessions within a period of eleven weeks.

Mark was not the same person I had known previously. I am sure pastoral responsibilities and opportunities have provoked his growth, but it seemed to me that the angel experience was pivotal. He was more direct, centered, and ready to move forward with his life. After our first session together, I sensed that, maybe, he was now prepared to deal with the big issue—his marriage. Here he was, a Methodist minister from a conservative jurisdiction in a depressed, lifeless, and probably loveless marriage with a wife who distrusted therapy, and especially marriage counseling.

Mark, a short, powerfully built man, was thirty-four years old and a student at the Wesley Theological Seminary in Washington, D.C., when I first met him. He had been married for four years to Louise who worked part-time as a secretary in a doctor's office. Then, as now, there were no children. He had been referred to me for counseling on the advice of a professor friend after Mark had confided in him about his lack of enthusiasm for seminary studies and his discouragement over "nothing happening in my marriage." The marriage had, indeed, become unfulfilling for both of them. Mark felt Louise's lack of attentiveness and interest in his seminary life and his plans for ordination and appointment to his first church.

Mark and Louise quarreled only intermittently, had sex on Saturday afternoons, discussed her work from time to time, and attended the necessary seminary social functions, but there was at the center of their relationship a great arid space where few emotional exchanges occurred. In a private session, Louise explained that she had experienced the sterility of their life together for years and could not get through to Mark. She said she had discussed the problem ad nauseam with him, but their talks never went anywhere. Finally she gave up and didn't see how anything could change. Mark, she thought, was mainly interested in preventing her from leaving. She did make two half-hearted attempts, but each time Mark remonstrated tearfully with her and she relented. Louise agreed with Mark that a separation would, perhaps, jeopardize his career, and she felt that she could not do that to him. She said she had a right to some warmth and love, but she despaired of ever having anything of what she needed from Mark. "He needs me and wants me, but it's like I'm his energizer or storehouse, and I don't get much back," she said. "I used to think that maybe I could fill him up and then he'd have something left over for me, but he's bottomless and it never gets to be my turn."

Louise had made it clear that she would not participate in

any form of marriage counseling. She thought that Mark ought to be in individual psychiatric counseling, and unless he proceeded with that she saw little sense in continuing. Mark could not accept Louise's ultimatum for individual therapy for himself, and after five sessions their power struggle over the issue resulted in termination for both.

Subsequently, I learned through a mutual friend that Mark was ordained and appointed pastor of a small congregation in southwestern Virginia. Mark and Louise continued with their marriage, but with little change, and Mark appeared as depressed and discouraged as he had been in seminary.

I sensed a bland resignation in this marriage, as if the two of them had decided somewhere in the recesses of their hearts that since marriage is generally not what it is cracked up to be and since Mark is a Methodist minister, they will tough it out and hope for the best. I knew that marriages lacking their own ability to generate voltage were vulnerable to one or the other partners finding excitement elsewhere with someone else, and I worried about Mark and Louise, especially Louise. She denied any sexual or emotional involvement with anyone else, although I remember being skeptical at the time and feared some secret third-party involvement might sabotage our counseling efforts.

In our first session after his return, Mark continued to be excited about his angel encounter and confirmed that he was feeling a new sense of urgency about his life, had energy he had not experienced in a long time, and very much wanted to do something about his relationship with Louise.

Neither Mark's bishop nor his district superintendent knew anything about his unfulfilling marriage, and Mark decided that he would discuss that matter with his bishop, with whom, he said, he felt more comfortable than with the superintendent. He did so, explaining that he was in a troubled and childless marriage, which he wanted to improve, with no guarantee the relationship could be salvaged. He discussed in some detail previous attempts, including the aborted counseling with me. There was no mention whatever of his experience with an angel. The bishop was more supportive than Mark had hoped. He said that if a good faith effort failed and Mark and Louise separated, and Mark's present congregation would not accept that situation, he would move Mark to another church forthwith.

Mark returned home to face Louise. He told her about the angel and his resolve to do something about their relationship. He said he thought their marriage had died some years before, but he wanted to begin a new one with her, and he was inviting her once again to begin marriage counseling. Louise said no, emphatically not. She said it was far too late; the marriage was worn out for her as it was for him, and she didn't want to try again as a clergy wife and certainly not with him.

It was final. Louise made plans to leave. Mark on the one hand, was strangely excited by his assertiveness in pressing his relationship with Louise toward some resolution, and on the other hand, saddened by the loss of Louise and the loss of his marriage. Yet he had no ambivalence at all about his angel experience. He believed it changed his life forever, in that there was a kind of essential "yes" in it from God—yes to life and yes to his life. He said he couldn't ever live in the kind of numb resignation he once did. The angel had spoken to his heart, and the universe had somehow shifted toward hope and a redeeming future. He felt known and accepted by an inscrutable and loving generosity he had never before experienced. Psalm 139 came to his mind:

> For it was you who formed my inward parts;
>> you knit me together in my mother's womb.
> I praise you, for I am fearfully and wonderfully made.
>> Wonderful are your works;
> that I know very well.
>> My frame was not hidden from you,
> when I was being made in secret,
>> intricately woven in the depths of the earth.
> (Psalm 139:14-15).

Mark is contending now with the grief of his failed marriage and with a traumatized congregation. His experience with an angel remains a very private part of his life, and for the time being he is content to have it remain so. Later he may consider what that encounter might mean for his preaching and his pastoral ministry. The immediate work before him requires all his energy, and he will leave the future in the hands of the Lord, whose angel proclaimed a message that liberated and healed him and, probably, Louise as well.

John, a life-long Episcopalian, is a member of a large suburban church in Fairfax County, Virginia. He is fifty-four years old, divorced, and the father of two sons now married with children of their own. John reports that he has an occasional "night out" with a woman friend, but he does not expect this relationship to develop beyond its present stalemated condition. He makes an adequate living as a lawyer, but his practice has not yet brought him the recognition nor the material rewards that most Washington, D.C., law partners come to expect.

Five months ago John began to experience back pain with noticeable muscle weakness, but he kept putting off consulting a doctor until his oldest son, he said, "nagged" him into it. He was fearful that he might have cancer of the spine as did his late father-in-law. Finally he saw a physician who diagnosed him as having multiple sclerosis. John was terrified. He pestered the doctor, he said, with the hope that the diagnosis was mistaken, because he had never had a major illness and no insurance company would ever insure him. The doctor triple-checked the test results and told him there was no mistake. John said:

> I was really scared, and for the next two days I prayed to God. On the second day I was taking a shower when all of a sudden I felt a presence there with me. I could not see her, but I knew she was an angel because she spoke to me. She told me that my disease had been diagnosed correctly but not to be afraid, because it would never be so bad I could not stand it. I felt a beautiful love and feelings of gratitude I could never, ever have believed possible, and no

words can convey those feelings. If this angel had asked me to follow her, I would have dropped everything and done it. Needless to say, my life is changed because I know something of myself I didn't know before, and I am no longer afraid. I think there are wonders in this world we can't even imagine.

My first interview with John lasted more than an hour and a half. In the second interview, John expressed an interest in becoming a client in my private practice. He said that he wanted to "dig deeper into this thing" and get some idea of where he had been and where he was going. He seemed to find reassurance in the fact that he would pay my fee and take comfort in the rules of a professional therapy relationship. Subsequently, I have seen John eight times. He has given me his permission to use his experience with the provision that he remain anonymous.

John makes it clear that confidentiality is important to him. He doesn't want his angel experience "diluted" by having to discuss it with anyone else, and he sees no reason why he should have to "put up" with questions from people who might want him to explain. John's reluctance in this regard is identical with that of Philip, Jane, and Mark. Not one of them, nor the majority of others I have interviewed, find themselves comfortable with the thought of congregational involvement in their experience. There is the obvious issue of having to explain this profoundly personal transaction to curious but skeptical fellow church members. John's life is changed, and he knows there are "wonders in this world" he never experienced before. But the wondrous events took place in a shower stall with an angel, and he finds no encouragement to connect that experience with anything his church has to say or to offer him. Why try?

John claims his angel encounter to be "the single most wonderful experience" he ever had. He says he never believed such an intense joyfulness could exist, but now that he has experienced it, he thinks his view of life has changed in fundamental ways. He says he now knows, really knows, that life can be worthwhile and that it can be beautiful. He says that before his angel experience he saw life as a "downer," and what one did was to make the best of it. He now sees things as "brighter," and feels "more lively—not so heavy. "

He is less fearful now than he was. John can describe the ordeal of his diagnosis in harrowing detail. He says that the life-threatening aspect of his illness is not what terrified him, because the thought of dying wasn't so bad. "We all have to do it and what the hell." What frightened him was the fear that he couldn't go through it. He would break down in some way and not be able to bear it. He is not sure what the "it" was, except that he anticipated that it would be terrible and he might not have the personal resources to "do it right." He reiterated that he was more relaxed about his illness, if for no other reason than his discovery that there was more to himself and more to life than he ever imagined. He is especially reassured by the angel's promise that he would be able to bear whatever his illness would bring him.

Reflecting on his career in the practice of law, John acknowledges that he somehow didn't make the most of his opportunities. He says he just couldn't bring himself "to go for it." He sat and pondered when he should have acted and then felt bad when other law partners moved forward and thrived. John readily confesses that his experience with the angel convinced him that something has been seriously wrong with him—that he has been "in the dumps" for a long time, maybe for years. From time to time he has moved beyond that downhearted state, but he has not really come out of it. He thinks his last big "downer" began thirteen years ago when his wife left him after an affair with another man. She thought of him, he said, as a "dud" who would just hang around and never advance in his career, even as one who graduated in the upper fifth of his law class at the University of Virginia.

John feels especially fortunate to have had an angel visit. He thinks he is "graced." He has, in some special way, been picked out. He has been recognized by this angel and that must mean, he said, that he has some kind of cosmic worth. John has never believed that he is a bad or worthless person, but he has never thought of himself as bearing any significant specialness. But now there has been a shift, and John sees himself in another dimension. Perhaps, he says, this visitation is some kind of summons. "Maybe there is a message in it to do something or be something." John is not sure what this might be, but he says, "An angel wouldn't visit just for nothing."

To use a very traditional term, John has experienced a *conversion* from one state of himself to another. There is a marked "before and after." Something is instantly synthesized in that one moment. *After* the angel visitation, his life is revised. His style changes, there are new rhythms, and indeed, the very cosmos is viewed in a new way.

John guards his angel experience from the life of the church where he is a member. Yet the character of that experience is more influenced by the church than John may, at first, be ready to acknowledge. His church is not an alien culture. His angel encounter has been informed by a lifetime of worship and instruction. He has been guided by a liturgy that brings angels and archangels to mind during the most sacred moments of the eucharistic action. Scripture is read every week and, as we have seen, the Bible is saturated with angel stories. And it is tempting to speculate about whether or to what extent John's enrollment in his congregation's school curriculum from a very early age may have contributed to his readiness for the angel visitation.

Equally important may have been John's exposure to a Christian message that understands and speaks to the precariousness of life. John's illness has clothed that message with its own urgency. He knows, as never before, that his life can be taken from him, and what life he has is not guaranteed but is given to him by a power he does not control and cannot command. John reaches for God's providence, and in a luminous moment it is bestowed on him with the ministry of an angel.

Experiencing the precariousness of life may move people to give thanks for the freedom and health they do have and thus be changed by their crisis. A pastoral counselor wrote:

> When my husband broke his hip last month
> he said to me that it was only right that for

once it should be his turn to go to the hospital. He was always very healthy, you see. He
thought that maybe his fall was a gift, a blessing from the merciful God, a respite, a stay of
execution. He saw how the prolongation of his
life and the reestablishment of his health was a
sign, a message from God's angel, and he is
asking why God is granting him this reprieve.

Our wounds may open our hearts so that angels can speak
to us, and their message requires a response. We are to live a
grateful life; but what one must do to express such a life is not
immediately apparent. It is here, at this point, where we meet
a central challenge of the church's pastoral care. "An angel
wouldn't visit just for nothing," John says, but what *does* a
grateful life include for him, and how will that gratitude be
expressed?

The church's ministry of pastoral counseling has from its
beginnings been informed by the psychologies of its day and
focused, as it must, on what is wrong and how what is wrong
can be fixed. That is a narrow, if necessary, purpose. However,
a wider, more inclusive pastoral ministry has always existed.
Its rhetoric includes other dimensions, the vocabularies of
*good* news, transformation, ecstasy, and gratitude. Today we
might call this a ministry of spiritual direction; although,
before Freud and the absorption of the insights of the behav-
ioral sciences into pastoral counseling, the ministry of pastoral
care included both.[1]

My initial interviews with John have led to some very personal and profound concerns. John wants to explore how and
where his depression infected his vocation and his failed marriage, and he wants to take responsibility for that state of
mind. We are proceeding in this task, but counseling John has
brought me more toward old, premodern traditions than I
thought possible. John's awakening from his dreary life was
precipitated by an experience he knew came from God, and he
knew that experience required a grateful response from him.
We are now in a kind of necessary in-between place, between
the powerful angel event and a discussion of what gratitude

requires of him.

It is my hope that John will find his way back into his church and a communal ministry that will support and nurture him. He needs the ministry of the whole people of God, not just an ordained portion of it. There are, after all, many men and women in our churches who know firsthand the transforming power of an angelic presence and would help if they dared and if they themselves were encouraged by their leadership.

Most of us *do* need a caring community and, for some, it is an essential. Barbara, twenty-seven years old, is the middle child of a Presbyterian clergy couple. Her father, pastor of a large suburban congregation, had died two years before. Barbara has been in the medical care of a psychiatrist since she was nineteen years old. From time to time Barbara hears voices, which she says command her to do certain things. She identifies these commands as coming from angels and claims they are the voice of God speaking through angel emissaries. Both her mother and her psychiatrist hope that Barbara can be dissuaded from this belief, and in that hope she was referred to me for counseling, in addition to her regular biweekly visits with her psychiatrist. The doctor agreed with her mother's wish that Barbara see me for "Christian religious counseling" and explained that she needed to learn how to ignore these voices or to manage them better when they spoke.

Barbara is a presentable and well-mannered young woman who holds a job as salesperson in the women's clothing department of a large store in the Washington, D.C., area. Two months before the referral, her mother noticed that Barbara had leased and was driving an expensive foreign car which she could not afford. An unannounced visit to her apartment revealed that every single item—kitchen cabinets, refrigerator, glassware, bed, nightstand, pictures on the wall—had been recently purchased. Barbara explained that an angel of the Lord had commanded her to give everything she had to the poor, which she subsequently did, to the Salvation Army. Then she went shopping, she said, and "replaced everything old with everything new." This included a new car, which she leased with a trade-in on a four-year-old Ford Escort. Her mother was appalled, made plans to protect Barbara from an impending economic disaster, and called the psychiatrist for assistance, and then me for help with Barbara's "angels."

Whether or not the voices Barbara heard were those of angels is an issue that cannot, finally, be determined by a psychiatric diagnosis. The authenticity of her angel experience is a judgment that belongs to the pastoral ministry of a caring community, and on that basis it can be said that the voices Barbara heard were not those of angels. Angels are fundamentally protective, and their ministry is healing and life enhancing. It is inconceivable that an angel would do us ill or command us to self-destructive actions. Angels are capable of announcing startling news, fearful news, and from time to time they do so, but the news they deliver leads toward the providence of God and that which is best for us. Also, the shape of the alleged angel message is wrong, and it lacks internal coherence. The voices go against the grain of biblical and church traditions as to *how* the faithful are to identify with the needy and give of their means to alleviate human suffering. It is clear that no angel sent from God would command anyone to sell everything she had to give to the poor and then replace all the donated items with new ones, including the lease of a bright red BMW 321I. Barbara is deluded.

Angels speak at the boundaries of our human condition, but they speak to real men and women who are prone to err, to distort and to self-deception. Teresa of Avila, a Counter-Reformation monastic and saint, wrote about its prevalence in her classic, *The Interior Castle.* Even our own human nature and our best intentions can betray us, she says. There is not much room in our hearts for many things but some tiny lizards with slender heads do enter. There are false and illusory angel encounters and love may demand a gentle yet firm confrontation when what one claims is, in reality, mistaken.

Counseling with Barbara has been moderately successful. She is willing to acknowledge that the voices she hears may not be those of angels, but she is not able to say, firmly, that they are false or illusory. She admits they certainly do put her at odds with those she most trusts: her mother, her doctor, and now me. None of us suggests that Barbara has been misled by a "bad" or satanic angel. However, both tradition and the biblical witness do testify to that possibility, and there is no conclusive evidence that it did not happen here. Jesus warns us in his Sermon on the Mount:

> "Beware of false prophets, who come to you
> in sheep's clothing but inwardly are ravenous
> wolves. You will know them by their fruits.
> Are grapes gathered from thorns, or figs from
> thistles?" (Matthew 7:15-16).

The fruit produced by Barbara's disastrous misjudgment was tainted, to say the least. Yet there is a pastoral imperative here. Barbara could be propelled into a maelstrom of unwanted attention, controversy, and sensationalism. The *community* of those who care for Barbara and wish her only good must have the final word. How *they* frame her aberration is crucial; and they choose to view it as a psychological delusion and leave the question of satanic influence to more abstract speculation. It is a choice with which I wholeheartedly agree.

It is not a small thing when a representative of the church's pastoral ministry engages with men and women who hear voices or see visions they believe to be sent from God. In some cases, as with Barbara, they must be lovingly dissuaded from such a belief. In others, such as Talmage Bandy with the old woman and my counseling with John, the feel, the momentum, and the biblical and theological style of the encounters is convincing that the angels of God were, indeed, at work.

Even so, as St. Teresa observed, lizards do have insidiously tiny heads which they poke into our most sacred places. An angel visitation whose authenticity is not in question might be distorted by dangerous misuse. An angel's visit that is not liberating then becomes a fortress into which wounded hearts withdraw, effecting a blight on their own lives and those they love.

Bob and Cynthia were brought to my attention by a clergyman supervisee seeking accreditation with the American Association of Pastoral Counselors. The couple, who were married fourteen years and had three children, came to counseling with their pastor because of problems having to do with religion and church attendance. Bob initiated the session with the hope that "someone might straighten out [his] spiritually confused wife." Cynthia was reluctant to participate in any counseling involving the pastor but agreed to three sessions because, she said, "Bob bribed me with the promise we would have dinner out before or after the counseling sessions."

Bob is a deeply devout person who attends church services regularly. During an initial counseling session alone, Bob confided that seventeen years previously—three years before his marriage to Cynthia—he had been visited by an angel, and the experience profoundly changed his life. He said he had then become a religious person "who wanted to know more about God and Christ the Lord." He acknowledged that since his marriage he and Cynthia had come to very different "world views"; since she was uninterested in religion and went to church only grudgingly, he had never seriously considered telling her about the angel visitation. Cynthia said, in her private interview that she thought she had a "right to be an unbeliever" and was coming more and more to that conviction the longer she lived with Bob, whom she described in an angry outburst as "a religious fanatic."

In a supervision session the pastor said he knew that Cynthia questioned his impartiality, but he didn't know how to build trust, given her antipathy toward him and the church. I suggested that he ask her what she did when Bob attended services. When questioned, Cynthia replied that she read magazines, watched TV, and felt angry and bored "because God and the church have him and I don't get anything." The pastor observed that she sounded jealous and guessed she was lonely and wanted more intimacy with Bob. Cynthia became animated, agreed that such was the case, and said that since the birth of their first child she had been "left to be a mother" when she longed for something more in her marriage, but it never came to pass. She said they just seemed to be involved in different things: "He got more religious and I got more motherhood."

During the third, and presumably final counseling session, the pastor said he thought they had spent too much time and energy struggling over God and the church and not enough time with each other. He suggested that their counseling contract be extended to include six sessions together, during which they would talk about their differences in more personal terms. Cynthia and Bob readily agreed.

A breakthrough came in the fifth session when Bob, with some difficulty, began to talk about his encounter with the angel. He said that although this was the single most important experience in his life, he never saw any need to "make anyone understand it or believe it." He knew it happened, he said, "and that was all that mattered because I want to hold this in my heart forever and ever." He said that before the angel came to visit, his life had been "a mess." After graduation from college he had gotten deeply involved in a love affair with a married woman, who became pregnant with his child. He said they were not prepared for her divorce and their marriage, and an abortion was planned. The angel experience occurred directly after the abortion. It included a warning from the angel that the relationship was wrong and he should bring it to an end. Six months later, at his instigation, with much pain for both and with some recrimination, they parted.

It was then that Cynthia heard this story for the first time. Her feelings were confused, alternating between resentment that Bob had withheld such important personal information from her and gratitude that he had now shared it with her. She was curious about the affair and was able to express some admiration for Bob "since he stood alongside this woman right through the abortion ordeal." Most particularly, Cynthia wanted to hear every detail of the angel experience, how Bob's life was changed, and how it moved him to want a relationship with her. After that fifth session Bob and Cynthia talked at home, they said, nonstop until 2:00 A.M.

At their last session three months later, Cynthia said that Bob's confession was like "a great gift." Although many of their "religious" differences continue to exist, they are softened. The intensities and fears that prevented their discussion are dissipated, and both Cynthia and Bob report a better feeling about themselves and each other. Later, in a private conversation with the pastor, Cynthia remarked that she had friendly feelings toward the angel— "because I think Bob and I are right for each other and we can be happily married."

*Notes*

1. History knows no absolute discontinuities, but the pastoral ministry of the church underwent a swift transition since the advent of modern psychiatry and the identification of personal abnormality as a *medical* issue. For a further discussion of this change see: Clebsch, W. and Jaekle. C. *Pastoral Care in Historical Perspective*, Northvale, New Jersey and London, Jason Aronson Inc., The Masterwork Series, 1994.

# CHAPTER VII

# Can Angels Go Home Again?

Can angels go home again? Can they return to the lives of real people *within* congregations and churches from which they have been absent for so very long? Does their return make a difference, and if so, what is that difference? These are serious and perplexing questions. Answers would be more readily forthcoming and firm conclusions available if I could mount more examples, preferably dozens of examples, to buttress a reply. I do have dozens of angel stories. They are not difficult to find and collect. What are, indeed, rare are angel stories in which angels do their ministry *within* congregations of faith and make their witness of God's healing presence known *there* in the congregation as the household of God's people.

I am, fortunately, able to give two examples as models for what might be possible for pastors and for believing, churchgoing Christians who may be open to a ministry of God's angels, and how that ministry affected the spiritual and personal lives of those who participated in these miracles of healing. In each case, courageous sharing within a small, caring community—a prayer group—was essential for the angels' healing ministry to be fully accomplished. It has never been obvious or easy for anyone to disclose his or her vulnerability to others, but good things can happen when revelatory moments break through among a group of loving friends. Members testified that these groups made the difference: "I needed to trust myself and my angel experience in the telling, and the group made that possible."

Howard, fifteen years old, the only child in a devout Catholic family, was referred along with his mother, Dorothy, and his father, Albert, to their church's pastoral counseling center by their family doctor. Howard, it seems, had staggered home seriously intoxicated, and vomited on the living room rug. His mother rushed Howard to the emergency room of the nearest hospital where he was treated, kept overnight, and discharged with the recommendation that the family, along with their doctor, look into Howard's possible "addictive problems." Later, Howard confessed that once before he had consumed an entire mugful of whiskey supplied by a classmate and had became "very sick" but managed to return home avoiding detection by his mother. He had used marijuana just one time and disliked the experience, and he had swallowed with no effect what he called "up and down pills."

The family came to my attention when the evaluating social worker sought my consultation, including whatever expertise I possessed regarding angel visitations, because that was an important, perhaps crucial, issue in the management of this case.

The very day after Howard had returned home and confessed his involvement with alcohol and drugs, Dorothy had an extraordinary experience, she said, with an angel. Sitting by herself in an almost empty church after praying the rosary and with Howard very much on her mind, she saw the entire church illuminated with a white light, so pure and bright as to be almost blinding. At the center of the light and just above the altar she saw an angel who seemed to be wanting to tell her something. Straining to hear that message, she said that her whole being, every ounce of her strength, was reaching to hear it. The angel did speak, saying just four words, "You are not alone," after which the angel retreated behind the light and faded from view. Dorothy said she yearned to hear more—to hear about Howard—but the angel said nothing further, leaving her with a statement at once mysterious, personally reassuring, yet silent about what she most wanted to know.

Howard, his mother, and father were invited to the first evaluation session. Howard was, according to the social worker, obviously frightened and depressed. Father emerged as the family spokesperson. Authoritarian, articulate, and sarcastic, he answered, corrected, and interrupted questions asked of others. Dorothy, unless asked directly, ventured nothing at all. She sat docile and compliant, with an expression of discouragement reminiscent of her son's. Despite the efforts of the father to convince the social worker that their only problem was Howard, the picture that emerged was one in which Howard was the bearer of family pain in a marriage riddled with problems.

At forty-four, Albert is a bitter man. After twenty-one years in government service, despite steady advances toward supergrade status, he feels that his work is not creative but boring and beneath him. He thinks that Howard has enormous but wasted potential and pushes him as if he were, somehow, a genius in disguise. When Howard does succeed, as he has with moderately good grades, and again when he helped to organize a rock band, his father belittled his achievement and criticized Howard for coasting.

In her own private session with the social worker, Dorothy, forty-two, overweight, and matronly, in contrast to her trim and strikingly fit husband, said she had a father who was never physically abusive but who bullied her into doing what he wanted and she was just afraid of him. Although she vowed she would have something different in her own marriage, Dorothy did what many do—she married a person with traits familiar to her, someone decisive and, she said, "masterful." Yet determined that her son would not be raised to duplicate such a personality she  encouraged Howard to be sweet-tempered and loving.

The social worker thought that Dorothy doted on Howard and babied him. When Howard should have been growing less dependent, his attempts to go it alone got no encouragement from her. On the contrary, he was made to feel that he might lose his special place in her affections if he persisted. Dorothy always questioned Howard about his friends, his interests, and accompanied him on every single visit to the clothing store, even to the purchase of a sweatshirt. Indeed, the only thing Howard was able to do entirely on his own initiative, with no judgment or meddling by either parent, was what they never intended him to do or dreamed he would do—drink whiskey and use drugs.

Howard is receiving mixed messages. His father wants him to achieve and constantly challenges Howard to stand on his own two feet, to be "manly," he says. Mother, on the other hand, delivers a different message. She wants Howard to be prudent, careful, and above all, confiding and close—the kind of man she now longs to have in her life.

After two sessions with the whole family and one with each family member, the social worker concluded that Howard was a mirror for the sins and failures of this family: a disillusioned and angry father unable to come to terms with his rage and who was in danger of losing his best resource and possibly his best friend, his wife who could give him much of what he lacks; and a mother who allows herself to be intimidated by his father and, to a certain extent, also by him.

The family is in danger. Each spouse stands stubbornly locked within their own personal dilemmas and each is hungry for what the other may be hungry to give. Howard acts out his family's dysfunction and the drama of their mutual deprivation. He is alternatively fearful, angry and apathetic. His shaky confidence in his ability to succeed on his own plunges him into desperation and the defiant secretiveness alcohol and drugs offer.

How to approach therapy with this family? Entering through the father might possibly elicit mounting denial and an assortment of resistances, and that seemed unnecessary, even dangerous to the success of therapy. The family had already over focused on Howard, and approaching therapy through him would only add to that difficulty. It seemed to me, at least, that Dorothy's angel experience was just the right point of access. Here it was, dramatic enough to capture the attention of both her husband and her son, and to focus on *herself* as a real person. And what the angel said and did not say provided a perfect portal to enter into the life of this distressed family.

Dorothy was advised to take her angel experience seriously as a personal message from God and to pay attention to what the angel said and did not say. The angel did not mention Howard at all and spoke only about herself. How *she* viewed her own situation in life was the issue and to this the angel spoke clearly. In God's eyes she was a special person who needed to be reminded that God watched over her, loved her and who was urging some important change in her life.

Dorothy was directed to discuss her angel encounter with her rosary group and to consider carefully how her friends there might respond to her. Her husband and Howard acquiesced to these recommendations. It was in discussion with this group that Dorothy came to realize, quite suddenly, that she felt empty and lonely and had, somehow, given up on her dreams and on herself. Her warm and nourishing group held her close as she spoke of her anguish. They listened carefully and supported a determination to begin a dialogue with her difficult husband about their real needs, their life together, and how they might become a healthier family.

Dorothy pushed her discussion with Albert into paths that were untraveled and distasteful to him, and she persisted. She had agreed to participate in couples therapy and she wanted him to accompany her. It was important to her, very important and she told him why. He finally said he would, but only because the parish priest strongly recommended it, and for Howard's sake. It was a beginning. Howard was to see a younger male pastoral counselor to discuss his personal and social life.

At this writing, Howard and his family continue therapy, and we can hope for each one's success. Albert must put aside his pride and be courageous enough to allow his vulnerability to emerge both for his own and for his wife's sake. Dorothy must welcome the angel's message in order to embrace a new sense of power, for everyone's sake. She must learn to offer her husband what he needs so that both can finally relinquish Howard to develop his own life in his own way. Howard must learn what all adolescents need to know— that finding his own voice in the world is a perilous process where he needs his emancipation as much as he needs his family, and that experimentation with alcohol and drugs is no substitute for the real joys and even the difficulties of growing up.

Jim and Janet were brought to my attention by the Episcopal bishop of a neighboring diocese. The bishop explained that Jim, a priest and rector of a small suburban parish, had come to him and confessed to a year-long affair he had just concluded with a married woman from another Episcopal church. The bishop said the confession was prompted partly out of fear, because when Jim told the woman he no longer wanted to continue she was very angry and had threatened to inform the bishop of Jim's sexual misbehavior and betrayal of his ordination vows. Jim decided to confess at once and to appeal to the bishop's pastoral grace in the hope of avoiding the more severe disciplines at the disposal of diocesan authorities. Six days had passed since the confession. There was yet no complaint or communication from Jim's partner in the affair and the bishop was inclined to think there might never be one. He said he was satisfied that the affair was over and had referred Jim for a psychiatric evaluation. He insisted that Jim tell his wife, Janet, about the entire episode, and that he and Janet counsel with me for as long as necessary to rebuild his shattered marriage.

It was Janet who called. She said she had experienced the most terrible day of her entire life and was on the verge of collapse. I offered to see them both that afternoon. They arrived agitated and confused. Janet was disheveled and tearful. Jim had the look of a man who was at once fatigued and exasperated. His first words were that he was at the end of his rope. He had done everything he could think to do, he said, yet Janet remained bitterly angry at him, "beyond all reason." Janet said she was undone by the realization that her husband had been "a liar and a cheat." She had not had "one clue" that Jim was unhappy, and she had never, for a moment, suspected him of "this kind of betrayal."

Jim and Janet have been married for nineteen years. They have two children, daughters, one sixteen and a high school senior, the other eleven and in the seventh grade. Jim and Janet are an unusually handsome couple, both forty-five years old, and under different circumstances they might have been depicted as a glamorous middle-aged twosome in a slick cover magazine advertisement.

The immediate, pressing issue had to do with Janet's rage and her obsessive reiteration of details about the physical aspects of this "sordid little affair." It seems that Jim's confession motivated Janet to insist on specific details of their lovemaking to the extent that she was embarrassed by the extent of her "greedy need to know everything—literally everything." Jim accommodated that need, with the unfortunate effect that the more concrete the details, the more lurid the account and the more rageful Janet became.

I proposed a contractual understanding between them as part of their therapy regimen. Jim was to steadfastly refuse any further details about his affair, and Janet was to have all the time she needed, within reason, to reprimand Jim for his betrayal. Jim was to listen without judgment or comment even when Janet's anger overflowed into shouting and insults. Both agreed to this arrangement and promised each other and me to abide by it.

It worked. By the fourth session three weeks later, Janet's angry outbursts were subsiding. At the same time, Jim's psychiatric evaluation had been completed and a recommendation put forward that he be in individual psychotherapy for a short time and then in a men's therapy group for a longer period. Jim agreed to these recommendations, albeit somewhat reluctantly, and began treatment.

Janet's violent expression of her feelings about Jim were diminishing, but her rage had migrated into a cold, unforgiving disdain. She said that while she could see some hope for not hating Jim, she could see no possibility of respecting him again, much less loving him, and certainly not ever forgiving him. She said, "My heart has turned to stone, and, God help me, I can't change it."

It was a painful and humiliating admission. Not only was Janet a person with high personal moral standards, but she also was a devout Christian believer. She could forgive herself for being angry and for whatever denunciations her anger might dictate, but what she found difficult to respect or accept in herself was a passion to punish, to "dwell on the details of this betrayal," and to find not a shred of compassion or forgiveness in her soul. Her hardness of heart and her regret for this condition lasted seven months. By then recriminations had ceased altogether. Jim and Janet were polite and cooperative parents, their family life marked by a quiet coolness. And although Jim was saddened and beseeching, Janet remained unyielding, sinking into self-blame and hopelessness.

Janet was a participant in a prayer group composed of members of their church, where Jim had been pastor for six years. They met in each other's house twice each month and offered prayers for each other, as well as others both within and outside the parish. It was with this group that Janet took a very great risk, which led to her encounter with an angel and to a reconciliation with her husband and the restoration of her marriage.

In a private counseling session, Janet decided to unburden herself to a member of the prayer group she trusted and especially liked. She did so, confessing her rage, her compulsions, and her unyielding feelings toward Jim. Would it be possible, she asked her friend, for the group to pray for her, the pastor's wife? She said that as far as her feelings were concerned she was stuck in a numb, stone-like place and she needed help, but, she added, "God knows how or what."

Janet's friend agreed to help. At the very next meeting Janet told the prayer group that she was angry and unforgiving toward her husband and very much needed their help in prayer. She said that the time had come for her to change and she did not have it within herself to do so. She was immobilized and out of control, and that was not good for her, her children, or her marriage. Janet found the group warmly supportive, and without further questioning every person in the group promised to hold up Janet's need before God in prayer from that day forward.

Nothing happened. The prayer group met for six weeks. They prayed for themselves, for others, but Janet remained encased in her angry resentment despite earnest appeals that her heart and feelings be opened to a new spirit. One afternoon Janet felt so desperate that she shouted, "Dear God, if you are really there, please help me. I don't know how to help myself." Emotionally drained, she went through the remainder of the day exhausted and depressed. A spiritual crisis was at hand.

That very night Janet had a dream. She dreamed that she was at home in the house where she had lived as a child. The house was on fire and in danger of being burned to the ground. Everything and everyone was in a state of amazing confusion, including the fire fighters who repeatedly missed every opportunity to contain the blaze. Strangely, every living thing, including the cat, her mother, father, brother, and younger sister, not only survived the fire but watched safely and without emotion as the house burned to the ground. Only Janet wept. She cried, she said, with deep, throbbing sobs, as if her heart were breaking. Off to the side, standing alone and with a regal and radiant bearing, was an older woman who said with a reassuring voice, "This is the answer to your prayer. Your heart is no longer hard. It is broken." When Janet awoke from the dream, she said, "It seemed as if the universe had turned around full circle." She said she couldn't describe the feelings of elation that came over her that next morning as she looked at the sky and the earth. It was as if she had developed "new eyes." She was overwhelmed with appreciation for her family and for Jim, and had a deep longing to be in Jim's arms and to tell him how much she missed him.

Later, Janet said she knew instantly that the woman in her dream was, indeed, an angel sent from God with a message that was exactly what was needed. She couldn't be an innocent girl anymore, always protected, never betrayed. Yes, thank God, her childhood house burned down, and she was ready now for a new life for herself and with Jim. Adult life, real life, came with a broken heart instead of a numb and resentful one.

Janet was changed, and her change had an immediate impact on her relationship with Jim. His participation in a therapy group had barely begun, and Janet was challenging him. She made it clear that her return to Jim was to be in a new and a different marriage. Jim, proud in his ministry of caring for others, had disregarded his own self-care. His greatest defense against the pain of his own loneliness lay in hearing the pain of others. Now Janet would no longer tolerate his evading his own personal needs, as do so many clergy, only to be caught unaware when they overwhelm him. If she had to relinquish her girlish innocence, he had to relinquish his boyish denial. She expected Jim to know what he needed and wanted from her and to be able to say it.

The challenge had a powerful effect. Jim began to acknowledge his spiritual exhaustion and his loneliness—a very difficult task for parish clergy when they are in touch with men and women every day. Jim discovered that he was lonely for a certain kind of intimacy, to be in a receiving, dependent position, to be cared for. Jim remembered that he went to see his friend when he, "felt like a vending machine that dispensed comfort and spirituality." He could never bring himself to tell Janet about his yearning for tenderness and caring. That seemed a troubling, even dangerous realization to have within one's family so he denied it, went outside his marriage, and boot-legged it with another woman.

Janet told her group that her prayer and theirs had been answered. She said that an angel had appeared in a dream to announce that a retarded part of her life had burned away so that something more mature might grow in her. The angel spoke with authority, was absolutely convincing, and, Janet said, she knew this was a message from God and she must trust it. She had been demoralized and had abandoned hope that she might change. She was literally disabled. The news that a healing power from beyond herself had come to Janet had an electrifying effect in the group. God does, indeed, heal the sicknesses and griefs of this world, and here was living proof.

One of the men in the group responded to Janet's angel experience with a confession. Seriously overweight, he told the group, for the first time, that he had been a binge eater for years and had consumed an entire quart of ice cream that very day. He felt "trapped," ashamed of himself, yet defiant about his actions. He said he hid the binges from his wife as best he could, but she suspected and remonstrated with him about his need for self-discipline and a diet. He "held her off," he said, by convincing her that the more she nagged the more prone he was to satisfy his cravings; but he felt "terrible about himself," even in "some kind of despair." He said that Janet's experience had given him heart to tell the truth about his overeating, and would the group help him deal with his problem?

A woman told the group that her marriage was at risk. Since the birth of her first child she had lost all interest in sex, and faced the increasing resentment of her husband with the hope it would "all go away." She said that she "yielded to her husband" from time to time, didn't enjoy any of it, and waited for the day when he would lose interest as well. In her own way, she said, she had an issue much like Janet's; namely, could a person be made to love and respect someone when one didn't, and how could *she* be sexually desiring when that desire never entered her head? She said that she was apprehensive about bringing this issue to the group, because it was personal and because she didn't want to "be made to do what I really don't want to do." On the other hand, she suspected real trouble in her marriage unless something were done, and frightened and stubborn as she was, she needed their prayers and God's grace. Maybe an angel would visit her. Another group member recalled verses from Matthew that suggest that when the kingdom of heaven has come near, the sick are cured, the dead raised, and demons cast out.

Janet had told her story *within* the believing and worshiping community. The Lord did this, she said, and that community was encouraged, their faith regenerated. For at least one woman and one man, hope was reborn out of the shadows of inertia, resignation, and despair. The outcome of their new affirmation and their reaching out for help is unknown. Yet each of them—the man called upon to relinquish an old and very destructive behavior, the woman whose sensuality lies dormant—is now on a necessary journey of self-renewal. Each knows that journey began with a gift, Janet's gift of her own journey and the testimony of how an angel changed her life. That it begins with a gift is, indeed, the Exodus story, the experience on Mount Horeb, the miracle celebrated at Easter, the New Testament stories of deliverance from the powers of sin and death. God is an alive and liberating energy today and has been since Scripture and the church knew his name, and so we are to give up our hopelessness, our despairs, and our resignations.

Miraculous healings were common in the ancient world, and they are not uncommon today. A recent broadcast of the Phil Donahue show took up the topic of guardian angels. Each of eleven participants told a story about a miraculous healing, a saving intervention from some threatening catastrophe, or unexpected good fortune that occurred as a result of the ministry of a guardian angel. Some who spoke were deeply moved by their deliverance, but those who watched heard not one word that the experience signified or pointed to anything beyond itself—nothing. Each miracle was encapsulated within its own individual wrapper and served up cafeteria style. What sets Janet's story apart is not the appearance of an angel in her dream. As the current media saturation reminds us, stories of angel encounters are everywhere. Janet's story is different because of its interconnectedness. The account of her healing belongs within a larger story, is integrated in the message proclaimed by the church and lived out in the discipleship of believing Christians—and that makes all the difference.

Janet's angel encounter is a model for a reconciliation between the church and those who testify to an angel experience. For its part, the church needs to extend itself pastorally, to be open to new forms of pastoral care, and above all, to make clear not only that those whom angels visit are welcomed, but that their *experiences* are cherished. For their part, Philip and Jane and John and Janet must find the courage to break through their isolation, reach into their congregations, and speak out. They have much to offer.

*Their angel encounter is a witness of God's care for the world.* No part of Christian teaching is more important to the church and to its pastoral ministry than a reclamation of its ancient view of God's providence: that we do not face the universe alone and uncared for but are shielded by the active nurture and sustenance of a loving God.

Nothing is so large as to be beyond God's care:

By your strength you establish the mountains;
    you are girded with might.

You silence the roaring of the seas,
    the roaring of their waves,
    the tumult of the peoples.

Those who live at earth's farthest bounds are awed
    by your signs;
you make the gateways of the morning and the
    evening shout for joy.

You visit the earth and water it,
    you greatly enrich it;
the river of God is full of water;
    you provide the people with grain,
    for so you have prepared it.     (Psalm 65:6-9)

And nothing so small or fragile as to be overlooked by it:

Are not two sparrows sold for a penny? Yet not
one of them will fall to the ground apart from
your Father. And even the hairs of your head
are all counted.

                  (Matthew 10:29-30)

Nothing is beyond God's providence, including animals:

But ask the animals, and they will teach you:
    the birds of the air, and they will tell you;
ask the plants of the earth, and they will teach you;
    and the fish of the sea will declare to you.
Who among all these does not know
    that the hand of the Lord has done this?
In his hand is the life of every living thing
    and the breath of every human being. (Job 12:7-9)

Indeed, St. Augustine, fourth century bishop and theologian, interpreted all these biblical verses (and others of similar persuasion) as authority for his conviction that God's care extended to pagans, including evil pagans and those who persecuted Christians. This thought left Augustine's flock aghast. How was that possible, and why did God love those who persecuted *them*? Augustine explained that God oversees the welfare of every human being and that Christians will often be confronted by wicked persons who remain healthy and thrive while they themselves suffer the worst infirmities. This state of affairs is, however, temporary, because during this life every human being must endure grave and bitter hardships. Yet Christians have an advantage:[1]

> we boast in our sufferings, knowing that suffering produces endurance, and endurance produces character, and character produces hope, and hope does not disappoint us, because God's love has been poured into our hearts through the Holy Spirit that has been given to us (Romans. 5:2-5).

Angels are ambassadors announcing God's care. They are sent. It is possible to stay merely on the surface of an angel experience, and some people do so. It is also possible, as both Karl Barth and Carl Jung warn, to identify dissociated angels with agendas more akin to personal idolatry than to that of the God of Abraham, Isaac, and Jacob. Angels are not independent spiritual beings but faithful ministers who testify that a transcendent God fills the world and whose reign never ends or diminishes, for "He who keeps Israel will neither slumber nor sleep" (Psalm 121:4).

*Those whom angels visit are witnesses to the transforming power of a new vision.* In our time we are beset with philosophies of change based on cognitive or moral appeal. The advocates for education, for example, insist that noxious personal behaviors, such as drug use or irresponsible sexual practice, can be managed by a steady educational process. Or psychotherapists will point to personal change as the result of insight and self-confrontation within a confidence-inducing setting. These approaches do, indeed, make for change, and, pursued with creativity, such changes can be statistically significant as well as personally profound. But there is another tradition about how change occurs. There can be an awesome moment when change happens in a split second as one is confronted by a new vision of oneself and given new hope. People are offered a new model of how the pieces of life fit together and where they themselves fit into that grand scheme. The familiar is then suddenly, instantaneously, transformed into something profoundly different. So it is when an angel calls.

Consider again the story of Jacob wrestling with the angel on the bank of the Jabbok. In this mysterious struggle, Jacob's life is blessed and there is a metamorphosis. He is no longer Jacob; now he is Israel. But there is more. Old patterns of usurpation and deceit are relinquished, and Jacob moves to a reconciliation with his brother, Esau. Then, "Esau ran to meet him, and embraced him,...and they wept" (Genesis 33:4). Jacob's tendency toward deception is turned aside, and he begs Esau to accept a valuable gift, not as a bribe but out of gratitude: "For truly to see your face is like seeing the face of God—since you have received me with such favor. Please accept my gift that is brought to you, because God has dealt graciously with me, and because I have everything I want" (33:10-11). It is in this spirit that Esau accepts the gift.

Philip barely escaped with his life when an angel warned him that he was about to crash. Jane encountered an angel at the foot of her bed and was told that God loved her. Mark met an angel in his bedroom, John met his angel in a shower stall. Dorothy met an angel at church and Janet met hers in a dream. None of them lived the same life after the angel encounter. "Because God looked out for me," Philip said, he knew that he must, in some way, respond. Jane said that her angel experience redirected her life. Mark gathered himself into a new resolve. John viewed his experience as a summons. Dorothy began to acknowledge her powers. Janet was called upon to grow up. An angel met each of them where they were vulnerable and delivered a message of powerfully good news: Look off your right wing and save your life. You are a loved child of God. Whatever you must bear you will be able to do so. You are not alone. Your heart is no longer stone—it is breaking.

And, a new vision invites a new perspective on ourselves, on our resistances, our refusals, our willful disregard—in short, our sinfulness. Mark is coming to understand how his separation anxieties are fed by a desperate need to control. John is beginning to acknowledge that there had been a turning-in-upon-himself that embraced a hidden sadness of wrongs committed and hurts endured. Dorothy started to understand that her disregard for her own personal strengths included a demand to be loved. Janet learned that a stony heart requires enormous energy, the energy of resentment, and without that one's heart melts or breaks. She saw her innocence as more than a simple lack that more information might cure. At its center lurked a willfulness—a refusal to mourn—to relinquish the certainties of her childhood.

*Their angel experiences unfold the church's memory.* Angels belong. They have visited men and women, igniting sublime and incandescent personal experiences for more than four thousand years. Religious men and women on the American frontier, and those today in our more charismatic congregations, may know the raptures of a vividly intense spiritual experience. What they may not appreciate is its ancient lineage, its widespread and Catholic antecedents, and the dazzling beauty with which the church celebrated such experiences.

A life-sized marble sculpted by Gianlorenzo Bernini, and called "The Ecstasy of St. Teresa," stands in the chapel of St. Maria della Vittoria in Rome. Completed before the first European settler set foot on American shores, the statue depicts how an angel pierced Teresa's heart with a flaming golden arrow. "The angel was not tall, but short, and very beautiful, his face so aflame that he seemed to be afire," Teresa tells us:

> In his hands I saw a golden arrow, and at the end of the iron tip I seemed to see a point of fire. With this he seemed to pierce my heart several times so that it penetrated my entrails. The pain was so sharp that I cried out, but at the same time I felt such infinite sweetness

> that I wished the pain to last forever.... So
> sweet are the colloquies of love which pass
> between the soul and God that if anyone
> thinks I am lying, I beseech God, in His
> Goodness, to give him the same experience.[2]

None of those I interviewed was able to communicate his or her angel encounter with the fervor and grace of St. Teresa; yet each one stands in that very tradition. The ecstasies of the spirit experienced in the revival religion on the American frontier have largely given way, in our mainline churches, to the bland, bordering on the dreary. Those whom angels visit attest to a very old tradition of great richness, which the churches must again claim. The rhapsodies that angels induce are, like the prodigal son, wasting in a foreign land. The time has come for a return home where they belong.

The transformation of life is ultimately mysterious and not immediately open to empirical proof. A casual observer may find that it goes forward very much as it did before. Philip still carries many of his old faults, Jane may display old disclaimed behaviors, Mark may move into apathy once again. John may never fully discover all the resources he needs to live with his illness and Dorothy may, from time to time, slip back into buying love with her compliance. Janet may yet cling to some childish innocence. Yet, each of them knows there has been a great change, because there is a new meaning and purpose in their lives. They have experienced a joyful sound, an angel's voice, and that transforms everything.

In these encounters in which angelic eloquence and personal need come together in one incandescent moment, a fragmented folk angelology is simply not enough. What is needed is what our churches have to give: a pastoral ministry, a place to worship with the faithful, the treasures of a long and ancient heritage, and an understanding of what God intended when his angel spoke.

The Latin root of the word "grace," *gratia*, is linked to expressions of gratitude for that which is a "gift" and "given." And the gift and the given are to be had without effort, and are free, so that they need not be seized but only received. An angel experience is not acquired. It is *received,* an event that happens, unintended and unexpected. Its center is something other than one's own self, even one's deepest self. Those who have met an angel can say that the experience *met them,* made something of them, and changed their lives. They know they received a gift for which no reason was forthcoming. It was truly free, but a gift does require a receiver who accepts it as a gift—as implying no merit on their own part. But what then?

For some, an angel experience is little more than a mystical experience signifying that something is "out there " beyond ourselves, but that meaning is suspended and unconnected. The Christian experience knows more—much more. Angels, Augustine informs us, inhabit the heavenly city of God and await our arrival as fellow citizens. Once dwellers in that city, we human beings deserted, sold ourselves by sin, and became wanderers on this earth, aimless and lost as one in a comfortless desert. Those whom angels visit must know that they are wanderers on this earth, where to pursue what the world pursues is to be guaranteed a broken heart. Angels remind us, Augustine says, from whence we came and where our deepest longings would have us return.[3]

The Christian tradition has always understood that an angel visitation does not stand on its own. It is a sign that we are not where we ought to be and who we ought to be, that we have sold ourselves into a spiritually inhospitable world—but we cannot buy our own way out of it, and that the incarnate gift *par excellence* is Jesus Christ, given to us by a gracious God.

It is the very heart of the Christian message that we are loved unconditionally by God. "By this the love of God is made manifest among us...," "While we were yet sinners...," "Beloved, if God so loved us...," "We love because he first loved us." Angels announce that message every moment and in every place and for every single person. They cannot really force anyone to live a Godly and grateful life, but they can bring a vision of a better way, of the good, the healthy, and the beautiful. They are like good friends, but in a way that no friend can be. They share our joys, our sorrows, our hopes and fears, and tell us that God is with us even in our moments of greatest peril and that God never wavers.

There is no final peace in this life, and angels do not bring peace where there is none. Life is off balance, in perpetual disarray, and what we know today we may need to unlearn tomorrow. But angels announce the very good news that while we travel this difficult world, we have been chosen for a reason: We are to live a grateful life. Those whom angels visit know, finally, what God requires of them—that they walk humbly, do justice, and be a blessing for their fellow human beings.

Four hundred years ago, English and Scottish Protestant reformers were fervent in their desire to cleanse churches newly under their control of what they believed to be pagan and popish influences. They whitewashed wall paintings, discontinued prayers for the dead, and stripped altars of their finery. Their reforming zeal was focused on anything that suggested idolatry, particularly the saints and the Virgin Mary. Carvings were burned or smashed, and few of the thousands of windows where saints or the Virgin had been represented remained intact. Not so with images of angels. Some reformers holding a certain and steady affection for angels, stayed their hands. That which could easily have been obliterated was not, and much early and late medieval art depicting angels survived.[4]

The "Angel Choir" of the English cathedral church in Lincoln still clearly shows very large angels with outstretched wings filling the spandrels between the arches. The angels represent the fall and judgment of humankind. Some angels hold the sun and the moon in their hands; others hold scrolls or musical instruments. One figure strikes a discordant note: an angel wearing a falconer's glove and offering to a hawk on his wrist a piece of raw meat, the leg of another bird.

The angel is tempting the hawk to return to him by offering a favorite food, something the hawk is sure not to refuse. The hawk symbolizes humankind. Whether orthodox Catholic, old world Protestant, or new world Evangelical, no matter, angels need not worry. We do return. Churches in the United States may neglect their angel legacy, yet there develops a vast folk spirituality in which their members have encounters with angels beyond their boundaries and beyond their sight.

At the funeral of a young man killed in a car accident one day after his acceptance at the Medical School of the University of Virginia, this poem appeared in the service bulletin, entitled "To an Angel." The poem had no author's name affixed to it, and it is doubtful that we will ever know from whom it came. It said what needed to be said during that funeral, but it also speaks for those whose lives have been touched by an angel and for all those who wish to have such an experience for themselves:

> Stay with us till night has come.
> Bless our bread, open our eyes,
>     Be our great surprise.
>
> Walk with us, our spirits sigh,
> Hear us when our souls do cry.
>
> Talk to us, the road does bend,
> Make our hurt and weeping end.
>
> Meet us 'fore the day is done
>     and heal our eyes to see the prize,
>     a joyful life in giving lies.

It was fitting for the congregation to say here at the end of that poem, "Amen, So say we all."

Angels were never fully banished from our churches. That may be beyond the power of even the most fervently iconoclastic. They *were* ignored, but here, in this congregation, in this service, angels were remembered where they belonged: at home again, in church, and in the midst of the people of God.

*Notes*

1.  St. Augustine, *The Christian Combat*, trans. Robert P. Russell, O.S.A. (New York: CIMA Publishing, 1947), 323.

2. Teresa of Avila, *The Interior Castle; or the Mansions,* trans. by the Benedictines of Stanbrook and revised by the Very Rev. Prior Zimmerman (London: T. Baker, 1921) 67.

3. For a more detailed discussion of Augustine's theology, *see* Robert J. O'Connell, S.J., *Soundings in St. Augustine's Imagination* (New York: Fordham University Press, 1994).

4. *See* Eamon Duffy, *The Stripping of the Altars: Traditional Religion in England c. 1400-c. 1580* (New Haven, Conn.: Yale University Press, 1992).